Bishops' Move

Wayne and Ruietta
Hope you will enjoy this
book!
God bless you and St
Mark's,

Michael Harper

August 1978.

BX
5009
.B57

Bishops' Move

edited by MICHAEL HARPER

HODDER AND STOUGHTON
LONDON   SYDNEY   AUCKLAND   TORONTO

WITHDRAWN
HIEBERT LIBRARY
Fresno Pacific College - M. B. Seminary
Fresno, Calif. 93702

110755

Copyright © 1978: Introduction by Michael Harper; Chapter 1 by Bill Burnett; Chapter 2 by David Pytches; Chapter 3 by William Frey; Chapter 4 by John Lewis; Chapter 5 by Richard Hare; Chapter 6 by Chiu Ban It. First printed 1978. ISBN 0 340 22798 2. All rights reserved. No part of this publication may be reproduced or transmitted in any form or by any means, electronic or mechanical, including photocopy, recording, or any information storage and retrieval system, without permission in writing from the publisher. This book is sold subject to the condition that it shall not, by way of trade or otherwise, be lent, re-sold, hired out or otherwise circulated without the publisher's prior consent in any form of binding or cover other than that in which this is published and without a similar condition including this condition being imposed on the subsequent purchaser. Set in V.I.P. Times by Western Printing Services Ltd, Bristol and printed in Great Britain for Hodder and Stoughton Limited, Mill Road, Dunton Green, Sevenoaks, Kent, by Lowe & Brydone Printers Limited, Thetford, Norfolk.

Contents

Foreword   7
ARCHBISHOP OF CANTERBURY

The Contributors   9

Introduction   15
MICHAEL HARPER

1   The Spirit and social action   27
    ARCHBISHOP OF CAPE TOWN

2   The Spirit and evangelism   61
    FORMER BISHOP OF CHILE, BOLIVIA AND PERU

3   The Spirit and community   77
    BISHOP OF COLORADO

4   The Spirit in the religious life   101
    BISHOP OF NORTH QUEENSLAND

5   The Spirit and worship   121
    BISHOP OF PONTEFRACT

6   The spiritual gifts   137
       BISHOP OF SINGAPORE

All biblical references (unless otherwise stated) are taken from the Revised Standard Version.

Foreword

'It is one of the majestic ministries of the Spirit to surprise us at every turn,' writes Michael Harper in his Introduction.

'Our concern is with the renewal of the Church, not the creation of a sect within the Church,' writes Bishop Richard Hare in his chapter on *The Spirit and Worship*.

'God does not demand an unreasonable faith but does demand a faith which goes beyond reason,' wrote William Law as quoted by the Bishop of Singapore in his chapter on *The Spiritual Gifts*.

If we bear these three affirmations in mind, and with them the insistence of St. Paul (in Romans 12: v. 6ff.) that such 'mundane' things as administration, giving to charity, and helping others in distress are real *charismata* of the Spirit, the Church of God will have increasing cause to thank Him for the charismatic movement.

Clearly those who have contributed to this book have felt the power of the Spirit, and their lives and ministries have been greatly blessed thereby.

May there be more 'surprises' ahead, and may we be open to receive them.

DONALD CANTUAR

The Contributors

1 *The Archbishop of Cape Town*

Bill Burnett (yes, he was christened 'Bill') was born in 1917 and is a native of South Africa. He attended Rhodes University College, Grahamstown, where he excelled in a number of ways, serving on the Student Representative Council, playing in the first team in tennis, squash, athletics and Rugby football, and being Chairman of the Debating Society and Students' Christian Association. A pacifist until 1940, he joined the South African Defence Force in that year and was captured by the Germans at Tobruk in 1942. He escaped from a P.O.W. camp in Italy in 1943 and was on the run in the mountains until he met the British forces in 1944. He studied theology at St. Paul's College, Grahamstown, and was ordained in 1947 to a church in Durban, where he established a city-wide multi-racial Youth Group. He did a post-graduate course at Queen's College, Birmingham. In 1950 he became Chaplain of Michaelhouse School in Natal. In 1954 he was appointed Rector of All Saints, Ladysmith, until his election as Bishop of Bloemfontein in 1957, the first South African born man to be consecrated bishop in the Church of the Province (Anglican). He attended the W.C.C. Assembly at New Delhi and was elected to the Central Executive Committee of the W.C.C. He was also Vice-Chairman of the South African Institute of Race Relations. In 1967 he became General Secretary of the South African Council of

Churches. During this period the Council produced *The Message to the people of South Africa*, a theological indictment of apartheid. In 1970 he was elected Bishop of Grahamstown, during which time he was Chairman of the Liturgical Committee. He was also elected to the Anglican Consultative Council. In 1972 he experienced the Holy Spirit's power in an unexpected and dramatic way, followed by the gift of tongues. In 1974 he was elected Archbishop of Cape Town and Metropolitan of the Province of South Africa. He has spoken at many Charismatic Conferences in England, Ireland, United States, New Zealand and South Africa itself. He is the author of *Anglicans in Natal*. He and his wife Sheila were married in 1945 and have two sons and a daughter. Like most bishops he has little time for hobbies, though enjoys landscape painting. Like John Lewis he collects artifacts. Like most bishops he likes gardening (and now has in Cape Town by common consent the most beautiful episcopal garden in the Anglican Communion). His wife says 'he adores history', but his pet abomination is historical novels.

2 *The Rt. Rev. David Pytches*

David Pytches was born the ninth child of a country parson and brought up in a huge rectory in Suffolk, England. In 1948 he began his theological studies at Tyndale Hall, Bristol (now Trinity College). After getting a theological degree (and after two years' national service in the army), he did his first curacy at St. Ebbe's Church, Oxford. While there he applied to the South American Missionary Society. After a further curacy at Wallington, near London, he went out to Chile with his wife, Mary, whom he met in Oxford. Starting in Southern Chile, they moved to an urban ministry in Valparaiso. They survived a serious earthquake (though their deaths were reported in the London papers). In 1970 he became Suffragan Bishop, and was appointed Bishop of Chile, Bolivia and Peru in 1972. He returned to England in July 1976, and resigned later that year owing to the increasing complications over the education of their four daughters. In 1977 David was appointed Vicar of St. Andrew's, Chorley Wood, Hertfordshire. He confesses, 'I love people and good jokes, but my own jokes are usually unintentional.'

3 *The Bishop of Colorado*

William Frey was born in Waco, Texas in 1930. He graduated in 1952 from the University of Colorado, Boulder and entered Philadelphia Divinity School in the same year, receiving his B.D. in 1955. He was ordained in 1955, serving as Vicar of Colorado's 'Timberline circuit' 1955–58. He was rector of Trinity Church, Los Alamos 1958–62, when the Episcopal Church sent him to Costa Rica and was director of the Church's Spanish Publication Centre 1964–67. He was elected Bishop of Guatemala in 1967. In 1971 he and his family were expelled from the country after he had protested to the Government over the killing of innocent citizens. In October 1971 he became Bishop of Colorado. William and his wife Barbara have four sons and a daughter. He is a consultant to the national Standing Liturgical Commission of the Episcopal Church. He has little time for hobbies, but enjoys music and an occasional game of tennis.

4 *The Bishop of North Queensland*

John Lewis was born in 1926 and educated at Adelaide Boys High School and Prince Alfred College. He served in the Royal Australian Navy in World War Two, and was in action in the South Pacific for a year. He entered St. Michael's House, Crafers, South Australia, in 1947 as a theological student and joined the Society of the Sacred Mission in the same year. After being professed in June 1951, he was priested in December of that year. He has held a number of posts in the S.S.M. including being Prior of St. Barnabas, Ravenshoe, 1958–60, Provincial Prior and Warden in Australia 1962–68, and Prior to the Kobe Shudoin, Japan, 1969–70. He became Bishop of North Queensland in 1971. He plays the guitar and likes folk music and *Sound of Living Waters*. He is fond of horse riding, and his hobbies are collecting aboriginal artifacts and relics of cattle and horse equipment.

5 *The Bishop of Pontefract*

Richard Hare has been bishop since 1971. Born in 1922, he trained during World War Two as a pilot in the R.A.F., doing his training in Oklahoma, U.S.A. He left the R.A.F. in 1946 and went up to Trinity College, Oxford. He trained for the ministry at Westcott House, Cambridge. After a curacy in Northumberland, he went in 1952 to be chaplain to the Bishop of Manchester (Dr. William Greer). After being a residentiary canon of Carlisle Cathedral, in 1965 he became a vicar in the Lake District and Archdeacon of Westmorland and Furness. He is married, and he and his wife Sall have a son and two daughters. His hobbies are gardening and (when he has the chance) making pots.

6 *The Bishop of Singapore*

Joshua Ban It Chiu became Bishop of Singapore and Malaya in 1966. He was born in Penang, Malaya, in 1918, but studied at King's College, London, getting his LL.B. in 1941 and being called to the Bar (Inner Temple) in the same year. He then became International Secretary of the Student Christian Movement (S.C.M.) until 1943, when, like Richard Hare, he went to Westcott House, Cambridge, to study for ordination. He was ordained and served his first curacy in Birmingham, before returning to Penang in 1947 and practising as a barrister. In 1950 he had church appointments in Penang and later several in Singapore before becoming Vicar of Selangor, Singapore, in 1955. He was Hon. Canon of St. Andrew's Cathedral, Singapore 1956–59. In 1959 he became Home Secretary of the Australian Board of Missions before becoming Secretary of Layman Abroad, World Council of Churches, in 1962. He was a Fellow of St. Augustine's College, Canterbury 1965–66. In 1968 he was appointed a member of the Central Committee of the W.C.C. and of the Divisional Committee on World Mission and Evangelism. In 1975 he became a member of the Anglican Consultative Council. 'I have no time,' he writes, 'to include hobbies or to indulge in them.' He is married and Wendy and he have two children. He has been a speaker at several International Charismatic Conferences in Australia, England and the United States.

7 *The Rev. Michael Harper* (Editor)

Michael Harper was born in London in 1931. He was educated at Gresham's School, Norfolk and Emmanuel College, Cambridge where he studied law and theology. He trained for ordination at Ridley Hall, Cambridge, and served his curacies at St. Barnabas, Clapham Common (1955–58) and All Souls, Langham Place (1958–64). He helped to found the Fountain Trust in 1964 and *Renewal* magazine in 1966 and was its first Director and Editor. He is an Examining Chaplain to the Bishop of Guildford. From 1972–76 he took part in the Dialogue between the Roman Catholic Church and some Pentecostal Churches and the Charismatic Renewal in the historic churches. From 1975 he has served on the staff of Holy Trinity, Hounslow. He is the author of a number of books including *Walk in the Spirit, A New Way of Living, None Can Guess* and *Let my People Grow* (published in 1977). He is married to Jeanne, who is the co-editor (with Betty Pulkingham) of the popular song books *Sound of Living Waters* and *Fresh Sounds*. He has spoken at many conferences and churches throughout the world. His hobbies are gardening and sailing.

Introduction

Anglicanism, episcopacy and charisma

Michael Harper

Introduction

IT WAS HILAIRE BELLOC WHO POINTED OUT THAT THE CHURCH MUST ENJOY GOD'S special protection, otherwise it would long ago have foundered and disappeared from the scene. God's providence has indeed come to the assistance of the world-wide Anglican family on numerous occasions in the vicissitudes of its existence through the centuries. There have been moments when some have been driven almost to despair by what they have seen and experienced in the Anglican Church. The fact that areas of our Church have been like this for centuries, and yet God has not allowed it to sink without trace, suggests some providential factors at work which at first sight surprise us. While overtly stronger and 'purer' bodies spring with alacrity into existence, and just as quickly disappoint, the old Church carries on in an infuriatingly make-shift manner. Many a prophet has forecast its demise, yet it is still here, and showing signs of new life all over the world.

The charismatics

One of the signs of hope is the influence and spread of the charismatic renewal within the Anglican Church. In his book *Holy Spirit* (S.P.C.K. 1977), Bishop Michael Ramsey, the former Archbishop of Canterbury, welcomes the Charismatic Renewal and hopes that it will be made at home in the whole Church. As far as the Anglican Church is concerned the renewal began in the 1960's. The beginnings in the United States were associated with the events which took place in 1960 in St. Mark's Church, Van Nuys, a fashionable suburb of Los Angeles. The Rector of the parish was at that time the Rev. Dennis Bennett. Although other episcopalians (for example the Rev. Dick Winckler, then of Wheaton, Illinois) had had similar experiences some years before, the happenings in St. Mark's were reported internationally, and Dennis Bennett became well known as a charismatic speaker. From 1960, when Dennis Bennett moved to Seattle, Washington, the movement spread rapidly in the United States and over the border into Canada (although its influence was much smaller in Canada until the 1970's). It began spontaneously amongst Anglicans in Britain in 1962, where to begin with its influence was strongest amongst evangelicals. Its effect has probably been greatest in New Zealand, where for example 50% of the clergy of one diocese are actively involved, and South Africa, where many of the bishops are leaders in the renewal. It is also active in Australia, where there is an Anglican Charismatic Fellowship, in Singapore, and in some of the islands of the South Pacific. In the United States, the Episcopal Charismatic Fellowship organises conferences throughout the year and has over a thousand clergy on its mailing list. The charismatic renewal has influenced both Anglo-Catholics and Evangelicals, and parishes of both traditions are experiencing renewal.

Does the Anglican Church have a future?

There are those who see no future for any of the so-called historic Churches. They predict the wholesale disintegration of institutional Christianity in the face of secularism, the collapse of organised social life and persecution on a scale hitherto never experienced. They have some grounds for such thinking, and there are indications that such a disintegration has already started. But the Church has always been to some extent institutional since the 2nd century, and such structures have proved remarkably resilient in the face of assaults from the enemies of the Church. There does not seem to me any evidence that the Anglican Church as we know it today will not continue to survive these pressures, and adapt itself to the changing world around. There need be no panic. The Anglican Church world-wide does have a future. We are not yet engaged in its funeral rites.

But it is not just a matter of survival, as if that is the only thing any Church can expect today. The Anglican Church has a unique role to play. It has always been a 'bridge' Church, a kind of half-way house between Rome and Geneva. Whilst seeking to reform its doctrines according to the scriptures, it never threw out the baby with the bath water. It retained the sacramental content, thus keeping in touch with Rome. It has always maintained that its bishops have remained in the so-called apostolic succession, a claim that is historically accurate. But what has often been overlooked is the strong influence that Anglicanism has had on the Roman Catholic Church in the last hundred years. John Henry Newman's conversion to the Roman Catholic Church in the 19th century has been likened to the Trojan horse of Greek mythology whereby Ulysses captured the city of Troy. Like the wooden horse Newman was brought triumphantly into the Roman Catholic world only to open its gates to the Anglican ethos. His influence on the Roman Catholic Church in an Anglican direction after his 'conversion' was probably greater than his influence on the Anglican Church in a Roman Catholic direction before it. Although Vatican I, the unfinished Ecumenical Council, was a set-back, Vatican II steered the Roman Catholic Church still closer to the Anglican. A worried member of Vatican II was heard mumbling angrily after a session 'this Anglicanisation. . . .' Not that the Anglican Church has stood still in this period. It too has moved closer to the Roman Catholic Church as the Anglican/Roman Catholic Statements on the Sacraments, Ministry and Authority reveal.

But the Anglican Church has not neglected the other end of the bridge. It has through the long period of its history, stretching back to Celtic times before Augustine came to Canterbury, been both a 'protesting' Church and a charismatic Church. Its long history (stretching back before Henry VIII, who was *not* its founder) is interlaced with remarkable movements of the Spirit, and a separatist attitude towards attempts at interference from Rome or any other foreign body. Its subservience to the Roman See was questioned long before Archbishop Cranmer, Hugh Latimer and the other Anglican Reformers came on the scene. It may well be its strong Celtic influence in its early days, but Anglicanism has a strong tradition of revival. One has only to read of Columba, Alban, Aidan and others in the early centuries; or the exciting story of monasticism, which thrived in Britain before the Reformation. Stand in the ruins of Fountains Abbey in Yorkshire, and you get a feel of the charismatic movement of the Middle Ages. Think of the Reformers, truly men of the Spirit, the Puritans and their influence, the early Methodists (all of them Anglicans), the Oxford Movement, the early Pentecostals, whose first leaders were Anglicans and who met annually in All Saints, Monkwearmouth, Sunderland, and the East African revival, which started in the C.M.S. Mission stations in Ruanda, Uganda and Kenya in the 1920's. The Anglican Church at its best is truly catholic, evangelical and charismatic, and thus has a vital role to play in the modern ecumenical movement. The Anglican Church does have a future.

Episcopacy

But this book is written by Anglican *bishops*. There have been lengthy arguments as to whether episcopacy belongs to the 'esse' or the 'bene esse' of the Church. It would seem that important though these questions were at one time, they are becoming increasingly irrelevant. To look at it purely pragmatically – the system, when it has men of sufficient calibre, works extremely well. When inadequate men are in office, it still works pretty well; and that is more than can be said for a lot of other systems. Anglican episcopacy, I would suggest, has some advantages over the Roman Catholic system. Anglicanism has tended to follow the Church of England pattern of parochial structure. The weight of authority and influence is tilted distinctly towards the local church or parish. The parson has his freehold or its equivalent. Although technically the bishop and the parish clergy share the 'care of souls' (the words 'both thine and mine' at the institution make this clear), in fact the reins are very obviously in the hands of the parochial clergy. The Roman Catholic bishop possesses much more power, and the relationship between him and the priests of his diocese is usually more remote. Thus Anglican clergy have the security their Roman counterparts sometimes lack. Good or bad prelates can, of course, override these principles for better or for worse. But the Anglican system means that the bishop has more of a supportive than a directive role.

Nevertheless episcopacy in the Anglican Communion is undergoing a crisis at the present time. In the last few years in England we have witnessed the early deaths of three diocesan and one suffragan bishop, and the early retirement of another. The system is breaking down because far too heavy strains are being placed upon men subject to normal human frailty. Some see the answer in making more bishops and smaller dioceses. Another idea canvassed is that bishops should have larger staffs, and be able to delegate more to their lieutenants. Some roles traditionally associated with episcopacy could be changed or transferred to others in the Church. One suggestion would be that parish clergy sometimes take confirmations, a ministry which belongs to Christian initiation and, as many sections of the Church are seeing afresh, should be linked with water baptism far more closely than it has hitherto. Bishops could also be freed from some diocesan committees, and able deputies be found who could stand in for them. When Leslie Paul conducted a survey among clergy at St. George's House, Windsor, 45% agreed *very strongly* that dioceses were too large, and 33% that there was too much administration. When it came to ranking the importance of the duties or work of a bishop the order they selected was as follows:

1 Pastoral oversight of the clergy.
2 Pastoral oversight of the laity.
3 Outspoken leadership in moral and spiritual matters.
4 Exposition of doctrine.
5 Confirmation.
6 Ecclesiastical duties (whatever that may mean!)
7 Scholarship.
8 Administration.
9 Representing the Church on major national and local occasions.

10 Outspoken participation in the political and economic affairs of society.*

As Leslie Paul aptly comments, 'it is a curiously protective assessment.' Anglican clergy are concerned that their bishops care for them, but we must remember that they are snug in their 'freehold'. If a group of Roman Catholic priests were asked to compile a similar list one would imagine pastoral care of priests might figure low on their list of episcopal priorities! They might be tempted to desire political and economic involvement for their bishops to get them off their own backs. But the survey indicates that Anglicans view the ministry of a bishop more in pastoral than prophetic terms.

Bishops and charisma

It might be a trifle cynical to point out, in view of the title of the book, that in chess the bishop's move is always diagonal, and never straight. It may move backwards or forwards, but never straight back or straight forwards. There may have been bishops in the past, who, in the spirit of what Anglicans have prided themselves in for centuries, the so-called *via media*, have said and done nothing particularly definite, nor taken a lead, but steered a middle course between conflicting opinions. Who, in other words, have made their role as a 'focus of unity' in the diocese an excuse for vague generalities which offend nobody and bore everybody.

We do need 'charismatic' bishops. One does not necessarily mean that they are to be, to use Colin Buchanan's term, 'card-carrying' members of the charismatic renewal.

* *A Church by Daylight.* A reappraisement of the Church of England and its future (Geoffrey Chapman 1973), p. 139.

But a man of the Spirit could be defined as a person whose life is open-ended to the Holy Spirit: someone ready to move and lead others into the open spaces, and into uncharted seas: a person prepared to take risks, as Bishop David Pytches was in his South American diocese (see chapter 2). We need to hear the authentic voice of prophecy, not the mere repeating parrot-fashion of radical shibboleths. In the chapters by Archbishop Bill Burnett and Bishop William Frey we catch new and authentic glimpses of what God wants to say in an apartheid society like South Africa and a revolutionary situation in a Central American state like Guatamala. It is not all condemnation of racism and tyranny, but the proclamation of the Cross and forgiveness.

The bishop's mitre depicts the flames of the Spirit. Bishops, of all men, need the anointing fire of the Holy Spirit. In earlier ages they often had healing gifts. What if episcopal visitations to parishes were accompanied with 'signs following'? What if confirmations and ordinations were the occasion for evangelistic preaching and teaching with a personal ministry to those wanting to commit their lives to Christ? What if afterwards bishops were to lay hands on the sick for their healing?

One of the almost hackneyed expressions of episcopacy is 'a focus of unity' for the whole Church. But it is a convenient one, for it directs our attention to both the office and function of episcopacy, which is to help the Church to find unity both with its past in terms of apostolicity and in its present reality in terms of ministries. However, the Church's temptation will always be to play safe and appoint colourless rather than forthright men, those who have little or no distinctive opinions about anything – and so can be depended upon to hold together conflicting viewpoints with the minimum of disruption, and to take an unbiassed if anaemic stance on the important issues of the day. What our Church needs is men of strong and well founded opinions who will freely express them in the councils of the Church, but men with the maturity and good sense to respect contrary opinions and maintain the unity of the Spirit in the diocesan family with impartiality and grace. It may be that this will require the patience of Job and the wisdom of Solomon. But needed it is, and it would seem our Church is not lacking in men of peace who have the gifts of the Spirit for such a ministry.

Some may object that one is looking for men who don't exist. But it is one of the majestic ministries of the Spirit to surprise us at every turn. Whatever faults the Church may have, dullness is almost unpardonable. The work of the Holy Spirit is not always exciting or spectacular, but it is never dull. He is amongst us to anoint men to creative ministries in the dangerous days which lie ahead.

The men who have written this book have discovered (in every case *after* being made bishops) a new dimension which they had somehow missed before. Such a discovery is not reserved for bishops. It is promised to the whole Church and to each member for his or her ministries. May we find it too as we read how the Holy Spirit began to move in the lives of six bishops in new and creative ways.

* * *

The chapters are arranged alphabetically according to the diocese or title of a particular bishop, not in order of the importance of the subject matter.

1

The Spirit and social action

Bill Burnett

ARCHBISHOP OF CAPE TOWN, SOUTH AFRICA

1

I HAVE FREQUENTLY BEEN ASKED TO SAY WHAT DIFFERENCE
THE RELEASE of the Holy Spirit in my life has made to my
witness to Jesus in the social and national issues of our
time. Significantly, perhaps, the questioners are almost
always people who are disturbed by the new emphasis on
evangelism in my ministry, and who seem to be strangely
indifferent to the way in which the Lord is renewing the
lives of countless people in the love and the truth of Jesus.
It is nevertheless a fair and important question, and one
that deserves an answer.

There is no doubt that the Holy Spirit has made a difference to the witness I believe I am asked to make within
the society in which I live. A reader of a Diocesan news-
paper, in which I used to write a monthly letter, has told me
that he perceived a clear change in the tone and content of
what I wrote after March 1972, and he concluded that
'something had happened to me'. He was right of course,
and it would be a very strange thing if the Holy Spirit were
to leave a man unchanged.

Both Church and World need the Gospel

The Holy Spirit draws us to the true source of social concern. I had frequently overlooked the fact that to exhort a
Christian to love God and his neighbour is not to preach
the Gospel. It is to tell him to keep the commandments of

God. The scribe who asked Jesus which commandment is first of all, and agreed with Jesus that it is to love God and one's neighbour, was told that he was not far from the Kingdom. A miss, however, may be as good as a mile. The Good News is that God loves, redeems and sanctifies, without our ever deserving his love. The Good News is that God values us so highly that he wants us to be his own beloved sons in Jesus the Beloved Son. The Good News is that Jesus gives you a heart of flesh for a heart of stone and as a beloved son fills you with the Spirit who will 'cause you to walk in his statutes'. (Ez. 36: v. 27). The Holy Spirit has taught me that to beat a man over the head with the guilt-producing obligation of the commandment to love his neighbour is not the Gospel. It is not the Gospel nor does it produce the result we desire. The reason is that men do not have enough love to love with. We do not have by nature the resources needed to live as children of God because our wills are corrupted by sin. The Holy Spirit convicted me of the fact that I do not have the quality of love which Jesus required of Christians when he commanded 'love one another as I have loved you.' (John 15: v. 12). How fatuous then to exhort men to do what as sinners they cannot do.

I perceived, however, that when a man says 'yes' to the love of God and is filled with his Spirit, he is set free to respond with love to the Father's love, and also to love his neighbour. The Holy Spirit both awakens a social conscience and conveys the means by which it is expressed.

Much of my time and energy had, before, been spent battering at congregations and governments for their failure to express love in terms of justice. I had tried to teach and convince by sound theology that the way of apartheid is inconsistent with the Gospel. A lot of my time had been spent on programmes to de-racise Christians. The results have been meagre indeed. Even some of those who identified themselves in 1968 with what was intended to be a South African 'Barmen Declaration', which would theologically demolish the ideology of apartheid as a way of salvation for whites in South Africa, seem to have succumbed quite easily to another ideology as a way of salvation for blacks.

The fact is that to attempt to superimpose a particular spirituality, a teaching on Christian ethics, or social action as an expression of the love of God, upon lives that do not know his love for them in Jesus Christ, and who do not experience the power of his Holy Spirit, is an exercise in futility. It leads to frustration, boredom, irritation and unbelief. To renew society with unrenewed Christians is like a non-swimmer trying to rescue a drowning man.

Man's Wrath; God's Righteousness?

I perceived secondly the reality of what I had known in my head, namely, that I together with all others share in a solidarity in sin. Together with that came the joyful discovery that we also share in a glorious solidarity as persons loved by God. This did not blunt my discernment of sin in myself. Indeed it sharpened it. Nor did it blunt discernment of sin in my neighbour and in the policies of local and national governments. But it did alter the way in which I addressed myself to them and spoke of it to them. We are not absolved from exercising a critique on government policies, or from speaking of and to members of governments, but we are bound to do so with love as well as in truth.

I must always have known that the source of our social concern is to be found in God, who loved the world and gave his Son for us, and who makes himself joyfully known to us as our Father in the Holy Spirit. But when I said, as I often did, that love can only be filtered into society in terms of justice, I really meant human love. What happened then was that my social concern became in fact a response to certain ethical demands. One then very easily enunciates some 'self-evident' principles and seeks to apply them with whatever sanctions or powers come to hand. The result was a pretty devastating kind of righteousness against fellow Christians. The means we adopt is the message we give. The message returned was something that sounded very like 'pharisee', 'hypocrite'.

In retrospect it is clear, moreover, that what I had to say on behalf of the oppressed expressed outrage at injustice, but I showed very little warmth towards the outraged. What I sought to do more often than not was the product of unresolved guilt. One tries to establish one's own right-eousness in order to qualify as one of the 'good guys' before God and man. This is unlikely to be God's righteousness. It is not usually an expression of the love of Jesus. One remains part of the disease oneself. I know now that it is better to speak out of love for the underprivileged, but also to love them with the love God gives us in Jesus. It is true that the Holy Spirit may give a prophetic word of judge-ment which must be spoken, but I have discovered that his word is as likely as not a word of encouragement and consolation. In holy scripture prophecy is more often encouragement than denunciation and doom. I find moreover that what I perceive to be God's righteousness is not as simplistic as my own and that of other men. 'There is a wideness in God's mercy' which eludes us. But it is precisely this which we experience through his Holy Spirit so that we become not only recipients of his mercy but also dispensers of it.

It is perhaps worth observing that it was human righteous-ness that was responsible for the death of the Lord

Jesus. It was not in the first instance the power of the state that caused his death. It was not disreputable criminal elements who caused it. It was the 'righteous ones' within the household of God. There are two good reasons why a Christian leader should see this clearly. The first is because he needs to be careful not to speak and act glibly from a righteousness which he does not possess. The Father gave us the Son 'so that in him we might become the righteousness of God'. (2 Cor. 5: v. 21). The righteousness to which we give expression is the righteousness that is in Jesus. We need to be sure therefore that this is what we are doing, and that he wants us to do it, before we speak or act. The second reason is that we may be sure there will almost always be the righteous accusers of the brethren in the household of God, and we should not expect to be treated any more lightly than the Lord in whom we serve.

Being a white South African Christian abroad during the last decade has often been a painful experience precisely because one sometimes moves among the 'righteous'. It does him no harm to be made to feel as expendable as blacks are in his own country. It helps him to feel how blacks feel at home to be given the pariah treatment by fellow Christians. Why do I share in this way what I have never shared before? I do so in order to make the point that the Holy Spirit is not quite as simplistic as our own righteousness. I have found myself lovingly accepted at international 'charismatic' conferences not because I do not in some sense share the sin of my people, but because in the wideness of God's mercy I am also in Christ acceptable to him. Because the Holy Spirit sheds abroad in our hearts the love of God, those who are filled with him can love the unlovable in a way I have not previously experienced. For that also I praise God. I have found that men are far more likely to respond in repentance if we love them with the love of Jesus than if we snub them or hammer them into the ground with our condemnation. In this also the Gospel has resources for the healing of the nations.

Shalom

Thirdly I have come to understand more clearly the social significance of the eucharistic community. The kiss of peace at the Holy Eucharist has become in many places of worship a joyful and authentic embrace to express mutual acceptance in Jesus Christ. It frequently becomes the moment of forgiveness and reconciliation. All that is solid gain. But what would love for the brethren mean if the person you embrace and for whom you seek God's peace has had his house burnt down, leaving a destitute family on the street? It is only the true love of Jesus if those who pray for the shalom of God to rest upon others become the means by which their brethren are delivered from anxiety and destitution. Where we are serious about seeking the peace of God for our neighbour, the Eucharist will stop where such a need is discovered until some sort of plan is made to bring God's healing where it is required.

The Holy Spirit sets us free to know one another as beloved in Jesus Christ. In the context of the Holy Eucharist he brings this home to us again and again. We are much more likely to care for one another when we know what it really means to be a eucharistic Community in the Holy Spirit. Because the Eucharist becomes in this way a more intimate experience it is seen to be all the more scandalous that some of us should be hungry and others surfeited with good things. Then the acceptance of gross inequalities and discrimination against some of our brothers in Jesus becomes ugly indeed, unless we seek ways to enable them to share in the educational and economic opportunities we may enjoy. When we meet to celebrate our acceptance as sons and daughters in Jesus, and become identified with the Lord who gave and still gives himself, his Body and Blood to us, how can we withhold from one another ourselves, our possessions and those things in which we have been blessed?

We need to be delivered from the breathless series of services to be got through on a Sunday morning, each with its allotted hour! Then the Eucharist can become the place where God does business with his people. Then in the context of the word and the sacrament we may have time to face our responsibility for one another in the Body of Christ and begin to see how God wants us to bring his healing to the world.

It is good to see that the Holy Spirit is leading us in this direction. In the past, times of crisis produced the loud cry, 'What is the Church doing about it?' By this was meant, what is the Chapter, the Diocesan Council or the Bishop doing about it? This is frequently an irresponsible and faithless response. The question should be 'What does the Lord want us to do about it?' During the riots in Cape Town in 1976 one of the congregations on the Cape Flats which is experiencing a renewal in the Holy Spirit was led to respond to the need of the people in the parish without appeals for help either to the rector or to the Bishop. The leaders of the many house groups went into action to meet the immediate financial needs of families where a breadwinner was jailed or killed and gave both spiritual and material support whether those who had suffered were parishioners or not. This is the Church responding faithfully to its social responsibilities. From their focal point in adoration, praise and worship; the faithful moved out to care for their own members and then beyond them to those outside the congregation. The next step is to plan action to seek to change the system in local, regional and, it may be, national governments where Christians have the freedom to do so.

It is when we take this step that we face the immense danger of being once again trapped into subjection to the 'principalities and powers' (Col. 2: v. 15) that rule the world. We will escape this only if we know and experience that Jesus is Lord because he is manifesting his love and his truth to us and in us by the Holy Spirit. In order to be sustained in this life in the Holy Spirit, we need both the intimate fellowship of the faithful in prayer and mutual correction, but also praise and adoration of God in worship.

The Role of Ideology

A further conviction of the Holy Spirit is that we may be far more deeply the prisoners of ideology (and the powers) than we think we are, and that this is revealed to us because He reveals Jesus as the Way and the Truth. I have known Christians who are renewed in the Holy Spirit and some Pentecostal Christians who do not see that they have a responsibility to society. They nestle happily and uncritically within an ideology which allows a vast gap between rich and poor and built-in discrimination against the under-privileged. This is depressing but true. Not only individuals but as far as may be, the society in which we live must reflect the reign of Christ. Otherwise we fail to fulfil the commandment of Christ 'to love one another as I have loved you'. To obey the Lord's command may mean for some a rigorous participation in politics. One of the results of renewal in the Holy Spirit for a man of my acquaintance was that he stood for election for a progressive political party at the following election.

If on the other hand we do not expect God to change people's lives and attitudes by the power of the Holy Spirit we cease to believe he has that sort of power. This is why many have, I suspect, drifted into a secular theology and even a theology of the death of God. To all intents and purposes He is dead if we do not ever see clear evidence of his vitality as he grasps and renews men by his own Spirit. Then all that is left to us is to search for change by means of ideologies. We must propagate the best and truest ideology. Then we must plan pressure groups and educational programmes to propagate our way. We become engrossed by our just solution to our problems to which we are now fully committed. And so we give a finality to our solution which it can never have and which belongs to God alone. This is why Christians are frequently not in fellowship with one another. If we have given a finality to a particular political 'solution' anyone who gets in the way must either be disposed of or at least beaten into insensibility. Then the liberal becomes illiberal and the moderate immoderate in his hating. This is simply a sign that we have become slaves of an ideology rather than slaves of Jesus Christ! (Unreserved loyalty to a particular Christian tradition of worship and churchmanship may similarly be an enslavement to an ideological position).

When, moreover, we use ideology, either ecclesiastical or political, as a way of salvation, it means at once that we no longer believe in the power of God as the only way of salvation. It is true that we cannot do without ideologies which are simply the systematisation of theological or political ideas in order to focus men's minds on a particular matter. Governments must have policies. Churches must describe and teach what they believe in theological terms, but none of these is ever more than contingent, God alone is God.

The opening verse of Psalm 138 expresses clearly where I believe the Holy Spirit leads Christians to stand in relationship to the powers by which politicians and sometimes ecclesiastics try to do what must be done. 'I will give thee thanks, O Lord, with my whole heart; before the gods I give thee praise.' The gods are by no means dead. In fact we may use their powers, but only as they are subordinated to the Lord. In the Holy Spirit we retain our freedom to use these powers and ideologies if we are giving God thanks with a whole heart. Then also we can blithely sing God's praise in the presence of these gods. It is a way of keeping the gods in a proper subservience, for God alone is worthy of our loyalty and praise. (Col. 1: vv.15,16).

Along with an almost embarrassing freedom not to take ecclesiastical structures too seriously, the Holy Spirit seems to lead the sons of God into a freedom to sit lightly on human loyalties and political movements. We cannot take such things too seriously because we know what is in man and that his solutions are never real solutions. We know, moreover, that in all predicaments, whether of revolution and civil war or of dictatorship, God remains God. We do not have to collapse in helpless rage, or be fearful or despairing. He is Alpha and Omega – the first and the last word to be spoken. He alone is God.

The Impotence of the Church

Every Christian has a calling to be a sign of the Kingdom. He is to be the evidence that in Jesus alone we may triumph over the dislocations of human life. He is a man who acknowledges that Jesus is Lord by the commitment of his own mind, body and spirit to the Father through Jesus. In his own way he affirms in his own flesh that Jesus alone is the Way, the Truth and the Life. But a Christian can never be content to remain, so to speak, in the singular. He is meant to multiply. Almost the first thing Jesus did after the Father anointed him with the Holy Spirit and he began his ministry, was to call some men to be with him. And so it should not surprise us that John wrote, 'that which we have seen and heard we proclaim also to you, so that you may have fellowship with us; and our fellowship is with the Father and the Son Jesus Christ. And we are writing this that your joy may be complete.' (1 John 1: vv. 3, 4). Being a Christian is an individual's response to God within a social context. He belongs to a community of those who have been redeemed through Jesus and shares as a son in the fellowship (*koinōnia*) of the Holy Spirit. (2 Cor. 13: v. 14). By the quality of its life in the *koinōnia* of the Spirit, the Church is to be a sign of the kingdom of God. Because we are a society, our witness essentially has social implications.

What I have written is, I believe, theologically sound. But that does not do very much to convince anyone that the kingdom is here. Many years of struggling with what it means to be the Church in an apartheid society has convinced me of the almost complete impotence of the Church to which the Risen Lord addressed the promise 'you shall receive power when the Holy Spirit has come upon you; and you shall be my witnesses in Jerusalem and in all Judea and in Samaria and to the end of the earth.' (Acts 1: v. 8). The Church I know seemed helpless to make a substantial witness to the reconciling power of God, or to convince men that there are resources available from God to set us free from avarice, fear, prejudice and bitterness. And this is the same Church for which the Lord prayed 'that they may all be one; even as thou, Father, art in me, and I in thee, that they also may be in us, so that the world may believe that thou hast sent me.' (John 17: v 21). We are promised a *koinōnia* in the Holy Trinity (1 John 1: v. 3), in which we come to experience a fullness of joy which convinces the world that something extraordinary has occurred. God's new creation is to be recognised by those who know the fellowship of this 'Holy Trinity love' with that same love which is shared by the Father and the Son in the Holy Spirit. This is possible because as sons in Jesus they too become sharers in the Father's love in the Holy Spirit. Thus we receive power to bear witness by the quality of our life as a community.

Very often churchmen from abroad observing the obvious failure of Christians in apartheid society have asked me what they could do to help. Frequently I said in reply, 'You could help us most by demonstrating that unity in Jesus Christ which we fail to manifest here. Show us how to be united by dealing with some of the ecclesiastical apartheid in Europe and North America.' Unfortunately we have not received much of that kind of encouragement. Perhaps after all the Church elsewhere has little more credibility than we have.

Because we know that God wants every man to experience the reconciliation and peace, which he has given us in the Body of Christ, we are bound to strive earnestly for it in the society in which we live. Whatever causes men to be alienated from each other needs our attention. In obedience to God Christians will therefore be called to speak a word against exploitation and injustice and the misuse of authority by governments, and particularly if those who govern profess to be Christian. Having spoken such words frequently in my own country I have become increasingly aware of the dishonesty of the Church, which expects the State to give expression by its legislation to a way of life which we ourselves have been unable to demonstrate. A man without legs cannot reasonably exhort a legless man to climb a mountain. It is foolish to tell an elected government what justice requires, when the Church is not a community made up of people who act justly towards their neighbours, and so provide the leaven in the dough. If we cannot give expression to the unity which in our theologies we often describe with sublime eloquence, how can we expect the civil authority to produce legislation which nurtures reconciliation and peace? A leader of his people needs the support of an electorate which is prepared to make the sacrifice his policy demands. If we dare to speak of the lack of freedom within a one-party or totalitarian state we need to be able to do so from within a community which knows how to use freedom responsibly. It is difficult to speak otherwise with integrity. It is unfortunately true that not only is the Church in Babylon but Babylon is in the Church.

Theory and Reality

We are accustomed to speak in theological terms of realised eschatology. By this we mean that every Christian should begin to experience now what he rightly expects to know fully in the heavenly places. That is to say, we are to know *now* what awaits us at the end of time. But when we have rather ponderously defined realised eschatology as already enjoying the fruits of our redemption within the period between the victorious death and Resurrection of Jesus and his Second Coming, we are apt to suppose that we *have* realised eschatology. That fact of living between the 'already accomplished' and the 'not yet' of eschatology may describe for much of the Church what is simply a vacuum. It may describe a void where boredom, frustration and powerlessness reign. There it seems God is dead. It is when the Holy Spirit is expected and experienced and fills the sons of God with the power and peace of Jesus, so that we know again the truth that it is the Father's good pleasure 'to reveal his Son in me', (Gal. 1: v. 16), that eschatology is being realised. Then we begin even now to participate in his 'plan for the fullness of time, to unite all things in him, things in heaven and things on earth'. (Eph. 1: v. 10). Then only is the void between the 'already accomplished' and the 'not yet' filled by the presence and power of the Lord the Spirit.

The Holy Spirit is the means by which Jesus is now also Emmanuel – God with us. The Risen Lord gives his people the Holy Spirit promised by the Father, to make them, through his abiding presence, an alternative society, making visible the love of Jesus wherever Christians live. By being this kind of society all men will know that we are his disciples. We are not left destitute by Jesus. Through the Holy Spirit he gives us the resources needed to be an alternative society. We must expect to experience continually the grace of our Lord Jesus Christ and the love of God in the *koinōnia* of the Holy Spirit. Unless this is happening, we have nothing to give the world which it does not already have. But the Holy Spirit is not only an explosion of divine power – he is also that gracious Spirit by whom we are transformed as we praise and adore our Creator, Redeemer and Sanctifier. Our Christian life begins and ends in worship. It is this that delivers us from succumbing to the powers that rule in the world. It must be this also that leads us on from being to doing. The paean of praise with which the letter to the Ephesians begins, arises from the adoration of the Lord who chose us before the foundation of the world to be sons and gave us the first instalment of his Holy Spirit. (Eph. 1: vv. 3–14). But his mercy is shown towards us not only that his Name may be praised but also because we are 'created in Christ Jesus for good works, which God prepared beforehand that we should walk in them'. (Eph. 2: v. 10).

Worship in the *koinōnia* of the Holy Spirit is realised eschatology. It is a rejoicing and adoration of God 'who rich in mercy . . . made us alive with Jesus Christ and raised us up with him'. (Eph. 2: v. 4). But it cannot end there because when we are 'created in Christ' it is 'for good works'. Fellowship with one another in the Holy Spirit is fellowship with the Holy Trinity, which forms the dynamic centre of a series of concentric circles of love. This is another way of saying that God is the dynamic centre of concentric circles of social action.

The social implications of eschatology realised in the Holy Spirit are enormous. Where the dynamic of the Holy Spirit has been appropriated by Christians of different cultures or classes or races, what may have been a somewhat formal and distant acceptance of one another has been changed into a relationship transformed by the warmth of God's love. For example, some 40 or 50 people leaving a South African airport for a conference on the Holy Spirit and saying good-bye to families and friends spontaneously mingling and embracing and kissing good-bye across the colour line is a far more effective demonstration of the sub-Christian nature of apartheid than placards. In the long run that sort of love multiplied will produce better results than security police, stone throwing or bullets; or consider two white churchwardens in a rural parish who find that the Holy Spirit, shedding the love of God in their hearts, delivers them from fear and racist prejudice. They open their houses to black persons for the first time. They welcome blacks into the congregation. In a conservative rural area fear of the neighbours' disapproval is conquered. The social implications are obvious. Or consider a black priest, who is embittered by white hypocrisy and selfishness in both Church and State, and is being crushed by his resentment and is unable to forgive. By the generous love of God in the Holy Spirit he is set free to be human and to accept and love all whom God loves. As a result of his ministry many hundreds of black people have come to know their worth before God and are no longer paralysed by self-depreciation nor imprisoned by hatred. Again the social implications are enormous. *This is realised eschatology.* This is the work of the Holy Spirit.

Here we must enter a caveat. Experience has shown that the social implications of the appropriation of the gift of the Holy Spirit are not always at once grasped. The Holy Spirit provides a new freedom to hear and see what God asks of us in human relations. It can, however, all end in something very like an automobile which revs its engine noisily but remains in neutral. Some of those good people who indulge in a sort of spiritual pub crawl from prayer meeting to prayer meeting do not progress beyond a revving of engines. This is not realised eschatology! Frequently teaching and encouragement is needed to engage the gear lever so that the power of God's love can move his people into acts of love.

We have no excuse for mistakenly thinking that those who have begun to appropriate the gift of the Holy Spirit will at once automatically receive illumination on the full significance of what God has done for them. Those who are new Christians will need most support and teaching. The New Testament letters are written to Christians, many of whom have newly experienced the saving and sanctifying power of God. The authors of the Epistles nevertheless find it necessary to instruct them about the behaviour of Spirit-filled sons of God. If this were not so, moreover, the ministry of teachers and pastors, of which we read in the Epistles, would be superfluous.

Greed as a source of conflict

When Jesus died he was laid in a borrowed grave in borrowed grave clothes. This should not surprise us, for this was the man who said, 'Foxes have holes, and birds of the air have nests; but the Son of Man has nowhere to lay his head' (Matt. 8: v. 20). He possessed nothing because as a beloved and obedient Son of the Father he did not need to.

I have never owned a really good library, but when I was translated from Grahamstown to Cape Town a few years ago I was horrified at how many packing cases were needed to move it. I used to value my few books highly, and I can remember how often I felt ready to screw the neck of someone who failed to return one of my books. Simply to own a good book or something of beauty may enslave us a little and cause us to grasp a weapon in their defence. We are often not aware of how much we are possessed by our possessions, and of how determined we are to keep for ourselves what we call our own. I did not realise this until my values were quite radically overturned by the powerful but gentle wind of the Spirit.

Jesus said, 'It is what comes out of a man that defiles him. For from inside, out of a man's heart come evil thoughts, acts of fornication, of theft, murder, adultery, ruthless greed . . . fraud . . . envy. . .; These evil things all come from inside, and they defile the man.' (Mark 7: v. 21 NEB).

Jesus makes it as plain as a pikestaff that the sinful cause of social ills is within us, and needs to be exorcised. He also couples ruthless greed and envy with some of their results like fraud, theft and murder and also with sins like fornication and adultery! He says, in effect, that obedience to sanctions imposed by Church or society does not deal with the essential problem. Keeping the traditions and laws, or creating new social structures, is not a radical enough solution. Because we expect far too much from political solutions, we overlook one of the reasons why it is so difficult to secure them. Our acquisitiveness uses politics as a 'civilised' method of brigandage by which we try to acquire as much for ourselves as we can, even if it is at others' expense. Economics becomes a barbaric rape of God's earth. Unless people can be set free from greed, that is to say, from wanting always more than they need even when it is at the expense of their brothers in Christ, they will continue to struggle for power. Fraud and theft and murder more politely described will be used to hold what we have or to grasp what we do not now possess. If our political freedom is essentially freedom to keep and not freedom to share, it gives expression to a greed ethic. The ethic of the kingdom is 'give and it will be given to you' (Luke 6: v. 38). When our ethic is take and keep as much as you can, hoard as much as you can for yourself in spite of the need of your brother man, you must go on inexorably to protect yourself at all cost from losing what you have. Then many will say we might as well hand over to the materialistic Communists, because we are in fact as materialistic as they are.

Liberation movements in Africa are not, quite understandably, concerned only with political freedom. They are also motivated by a realisation that black people do not have a share of the economic cake that the soil and mines and waters of their countries produce. Greed is responsible for gross disparities in economic opportunity and rewards in Southern Africa, as it is also in other parts of the world. Greed is thus a potent source of conflict. Christians cannot claim to have made a noteworthy witness by their resistance to the sins of avarice and acquisitiveness. Many of us could so easily have been poorer that others might have enough.

It is disturbing that we do not readily recognise that we

who have spoken truly and rightly about the need for justice have failed to convey to our people the spiritual resources to make God's justice possible. What more than propaganda are our fine statements unless we are also exorcising fear in our people so that they no longer cling angrily to what they possess on one hand or are too afraid to assert their manhood on the other? How can our justice take flesh unless we have introduced men to an experience of the love of God that sets them free to accept one another as brothers and to forgive the unforgivable. How can we with any integrity talk about economic justice when we cannot lead our own people to yield themselves and all they have and are to God, in order to be released from the tyranny of being possessed by possessions?

The Gospel for the poor

St. John reminds us, 'Do not love the world or the things that are in the world. . . He who does the will of the Father abides for ever.' (1 John 2: vv. 15–17). We are to love the world in no other way than God loves it. Our loving may easily degenerate into so caring for the poor that we pauperise him and make him dependent on us and a despiser of himself! We need always also to offer him a Gospel by which he knows himself infinitely valued as the beloved in Jesus Christ.

Unless we also convey the Gospel of the sufficiency of God's grace to them, our cries for social and economic justice may well inject the so-called poor with the disease of our own acquisitive gluttony. The Gospel that Jesus preached to the poor in that much misused passage, 'The Spirit of the Lord is upon me, because he has anointed me to preach good news to the poor. He has sent me to proclaim release to the captives and recovering of sight to the blind, to set at liberty those who are oppressed, to proclaim the acceptable year of the Lord' (Luke 4: vv. 18–19), is not the Gospel of Jesus Christ if it fails to convey liberation from the worm that feeds at the core of the ruddiest apple, namely, the sin of that poor man who turns out after all to be Everyman. It is a glib and gross distortion of the Gospel to suppose that God's good news is only for the proletariat. The Gospel is for every man who has a need of the grace of God because he is a sinner. We may not set limits to his grace. To some it is good news that they can so experience the sufficiency of God's love in Jesus that they are free no longer to cling to wealth and power. To others it is also good news, that because God's love is towards them in Jesus Christ, He will meet not only their personal and spiritual needs, but also their material needs in a society that reflects the kingdom of God.

We may thank God when the pressures of history reveal our own spiritual nakedness and sinfulness. It is not simply that we fail to theologise aright or to understand God's demands in terms of personal and social ethics, or to evolve adequate media for communicating Church news or that we have not planned well, or have organised too little or too much. Our failure is that we have not led our people to receive the dynamic to be and do what we talk about. St. Luke quotes the tradition that the risen Lord said to his disciples, 'I send the promise of my Father upon you; but stay in the city until you are clothed with power from on high' (Luke 24: v. 49). That power is conveyed by the Holy Spirit who has been given to us. It is cynical and sinful to accommodate ourselves to the weakness and hopelessness among Christians, to which we may have grown accustomed.

I have a cartoon showing a camel groaning under the burden of ecclesiastical bric-a-brac and money bags being pushed by two plump prelates in cope and mitre towards a narrow gate in the heavenly city. That camel cannot get through the eye of a needle! And that camel does not bear much witness to the simplicity of life of its Saviour. The Holy Spirit not only convicts us of sin in this matter, but also leads us to utter a loving 'yes' to the Lord's request that we give back to him, for his use, all that he has given us. To be delivered from our possessions is a new freedom which is a source of deep joy. It is one of the fruits of the Spirit which St. Paul does not seem to mention.

When Christians live in this freedom they will joyfully tithe their income for the love of God. And because they will stick less tightly to their possessions they will provide a sorely needed antidote to the brashly acquisitive values of the consumer society. The Spirit of God not only calls us to a simplicity of life, but he also holds us in the inexpressible wealth of God's love, so that we find it easy to be divested of what we once thought was indispensable.

Thus we do not have to wait for legislation to enable us to do good. There is nothing to prevent most of us from using our material resources to benefit underprivileged people now. Only an awareness of their needs, and some planning, is required to allow the compassion which is God's gift to us through his Spirit to find expression. The means to do what God asks of us are available when, like the Corinthians, we first give ourselves to the Lord.

Paul tests pietists and activists

Let us be open to hear a word which will lay bare a foolish dichotomy in which some of us find a refuge when we face our responsibility as Christians in society. It is, I believe, salutary to test ourselves by what Saint Paul says in 1 Corinthians 13: 'If I speak with the tongues of men and of angels but have not love I am a noisy gong or a clanging cymbal' (1 Cor. 13: v. 1). This is clearly a word to those who exercise charismatic gifts but have no love. These are they who are gifted to speak eloquently in the tongues of men as God's evangelists and apologists and also praise God in worship with tongues of angels in glossolalia. Without love both kinds of speech are noisy gongs or clanging cymbals. So also words of prophecy, the discerning of spirits, sound theology and faith are useless without love. The man with a superb theology and noble principles of social justice, who is unable to act in love and forgive all men with the love of Jesus, does not glorify God. The gong is sounded, moreover, and the cymbal clanged by the Apostle James who says, 'If a brother or sister is ill clad and in lack of daily food, and one of you says to them, "Go in peace, be warmed and filled", without giving them the things they need, what does it profit?' (James 2: vv. 15–17).

But there is more. If I put my body on the line, work my fingers to the bone for my brother in need and give my body to be burned, and have no love, I gain nothing. (1 Cor. 13: v. 3). The man who is unsparing in the denunciation of injustice, and in raising of funds to relieve the impoverished, and in doing propaganda to secure a more just society, is far too ready to assume that this is love in action. It is frequently nothing of the kind. I know that because I have been there. It is easy to act and speak about justice and radical change because of your sense of guilt or because you have been humiliated; one can act out of envy because you are hungry for power, or to gain a reputation for being one of the 'good guys'. But if you still remain unable to relate warmly and humbly to the man for whom you speak or to forgive those against whom you struggle, you remain part of the disease yourself. You do not reflect the kingdom. You gain nothing without love. Let us not imagine then, that in our efforts to achieve their objective we have done any more than change one problem for another. I wish that many more of our Church people would be deeply immersed in political action for the renewal of society, but they had better not do so unless they are secure and soundly rooted in the love of Jesus. If they are not, they will remain part of the disease of our society and being imprisoned by the powers, they will certainly become their instruments instead of servants of God. I have been there too.

It may well be that we are all closer to the righteousness of the Pharisees, which Jesus said we must exceed, than we think. It is because the Church has failed to do its job of evangelising its own people that we find so many societies in a turmoil of anger and resentment and fear. Why is it then that so many of us who warn most ardently about injustice in our society and the danger of conflict fail almost completely to free our own people through the Gospel to respond to one another with the love of Jesus? Is it because we are so impotent to change people's lives by the Gospel that we turn to social surgery as the way to an abundant life. We will then find our people have neither the will nor the desire to accomplish what needs to be done or they will be moved to action or reaction by a dynamic which knows nothing of the Spirit of Jesus. 'Salvation belongs to our God who sits upon the throne, and to the Lamb' (Rev. 7: v. 10).

Why is it that those of us who are hot for evangelism so often stop short of teaching our people that loving our neighbour has not only an interpersonal dimension but a social one? Is it because we stop short of the toll the world will demand from us in sacrifice and even suffering if we take our social responsibilities seriously? 'By this we know love, that he laid down his life for us; and we ought to lay down our lives for the brethren' (1 John 3: v. 16).

The fact is that while they point the finger at one another in an imagined righteousness, both 'pietist' and 'activist' may be under the same condemnation. Without the dynamic of the love of Jesus, which is earthed in love conveyed and love enacted, spiritual gifts on the one hand and social ethics and political action on the other, are, to quote Jude out of context, 'waterless clouds carried along by winds; fruitless trees in late autumn'. Both are impotent and fruitless. Neither adequately reflects the kingdom of God. They leave the principalities and powers in control.

It may be, moreover, that as we shoulder our responsibilities to society we need to remember that by the same Spirit God gives diverse gifts. All Christians will not be asked to do the same thing. The role of some will be to establish good relations with the civil authorities and to work with them to seek improvements in the common life. Others may be called to be troubleshooters on the front line. Elijah and Obadiah may both be necessary. It is sometimes difficult to keep them loving one another, if each thinks the other should have the same ministry as he has. Do we not know that God gives his people a variety of gifts for ministry? (Rom. 12: vv. 3–8). But we may be sure the Spirit of God will make possible the unity in diversity to which he calls us.

When black migrant labourers in Cape Town attacked one of the African townships in December 1976 in a spree of burnings and killings one felt bound to blame the system that makes migrant labour necessary. The young people in the township, who provoked the attack, were also blameworthy. The riot police seem to have been blameworthy too. One is tempted to apportion blame where we think it is deserved. It did not occur to us to blame the Church. And yet our evangelism in the migrants' compound has been minimal. Our evangelism among young people has generally been ineffective, and the witness of the Church to unity in Christ, and responsible loving of one another so minimal, that it would not surprise me at all to hear addressed to us as we stand before the Lord blaming one another, the same word Nathan the prophet spoke to David: 'Thou art the man.'

It may be that by focussing on social and economic justice and problems of race, or the proper exercise of political power we have been deflected from dealing effectively with the sinfulness of our own human condition. Paul puts his finger with unerring aim on the real issue when he says, 'since they did not see fit to acknowledge God, God gave them up to a base mind and to improper conduct.' (Rom. 1: v. 28). We are in the first instance facing a crisis of faith. The real question is, *do we believe in God whose steadfast loving kindness is wholly trustworthy?* (Ps. 108: v. 4). The scandal is that the community of men which is a creation of the love of God in Jesus, who comes to abide not only with them but also in them through his Holy Spirit, is by and large impotent to express the love of God. *This is the crisis of the Church which is reflected in society.* And somehow we look in every other direction for solutions to the problem but to God. You and I are the problem not only our neighbour, the Communist, apartheid, the West, the Afrikaner, the black man, the white man, the capitalist and the labour unions.

The authority of civil governments

Christians must take seriously the recognition given to the civil power in John 19: v. 10 and what is said by St. Paul in Romans 13: vv. 1–7. The civil power is a gift to us from

God, even when it is, as it always must be, inadequate. The tradition of the Church recognises an obligation to give an allegiance to the State. This allegiance is not final. St. Paul assumes, for example, that 'rulers are not a terror to good conduct but to bad. Would you have no fear of him who is in authority? Then do what is good and you will receive his approval for he is God's servant for your good' (Rom. 13: vv. 3–4). But what if the State is a terror to those who do good? What if the law prevents husbands and wives living together, as God intends for the well-being of husband and wife and of the family? What if it takes away your freedom to marry the person God calls you to marry because you are white and she is black? What if the government has a manifestly unfair policy in the distribution of land and the distribution of benefits of the wealth from the land's resources? What if you are imprisoned for lengthy periods without trial, if you dare to work resolutely for changes which would produce more justice or more freedom for more people? What then?

Christians will give different answers to this question. Some will claim that a Christian is free to resort to revolutionary and violent action, or should refuse to defend it, where a society is flagrantly unjust and substantial change cannot be achieved in any other way. Others in the same society may well question the political judgement of those who reach this conclusion and believe that options still exist for peaceful change. Others again will maintain that Christians may not ever use violence to seize power or to defend their exercise of it.

Several things flow from this.

1   Christians whose convictions and political judgement lead them to different conclusions should deal with one another in love and in a spirit of mutual for-

giveness. Thus the Christian pacifist and the Christian who takes part in armed conflict continue to belong to us and to one another as brothers in Christ, however mistaken each may believe the other to be.

2   All Christians will discourage the too easy tendency to resort to violent conflict and even more obviously deplore and seek to prevent mindless violence.

3   Responsible citizenship requires of Christians that they apply themselves urgently to the task of producing a form of society in which there is little temptation to seek violent change.

Because authority for government is given to the State it does not follow that its policies are the reflection of the kingdom of God. Christians need to be on their guard against attempts made by governments or their political opponents to imply that their policies are those of the Church.

Marxist states which are frankly atheist may make totalitarian claims which will be idolatrous because they demand a loyalty we can only give to God. There is no question, however, of their disguising themselves as the representative of an authentic Christian stance and claiming approval for and obedience to their ideology on these grounds.

Elsewhere governments may have an unspoken alliance with the Church or may represent themselves as the authentically Christian way of life and so claim sanction for their policies which rest on a claim to be truly Christian. In the same way parties and pressure groups working to bring about radical change frequently seek to acquire for themselves the truly Christian stamp. They also claim to be the only authentic expression of Christian obedience. In both these instances we need to be alert lest we give allegiance to what is in effect 'a desolating sacrilege set up where it ought not to be'. (Mark 13: v. 14).

Although the civil authority may exercise a power which is given by God, and is thus his servant, it is evident for this very reason that governments must use power always in subordination to God. No political system can ever claim to be anything more than an approximation to justice or freedom. Because it is devised by men it will not only be an expression of idealism, which is frequently idolatrous, but also of human greed, self interest and lust for power, which are not expressions of the reign of Jesus Christ. Neither governments nor those who seek to overthrow them may therefore claim to be the only and authentic political expression of the will of God. Christians must be vigilant to ensure that they are not beguiled into giving an ultimate and divine authority which no State or political movement can rightly claim.

A crisis of faith

A professor is reported as saying at a UNESCO Conference, 'Writers, intellectuals, scientists and educators, thinkers and policy-makers should combine their energies to ensure that man prevailed over himself and created a climate of peace.' (*Cape Times*, November 1976). It is good that men should strive in this way, but we cannot by this means expect to prevail over ourselves and create a climate of peace. We think too readily that we can find our peace and our salvation in policy-makers, military power, sociology or a variety of experts. But the Lord says, 'Not by might, nor by power but by my Spirit'. (Zech. 4: v. 6). And the saints described at worship in the apocalypse cry out 'Salvation belongs to our God who sits upon the throne, and to the Lamb' (Rev. 7: v. 10). This is true because the problem of man is not simply lack of knowledge of what is good and true, but an impotence to act rightly because of sin. It is the Lord who alone deals adequately with sin.

The sin of which we are most guilty is not simply that we have failed to speak or act rightly but that we have chosen our own forms of righteousness instead of God's. Christian people are under judgement not only because we have been selfish or greedy, but because we have believed more in our own forms of righteousness and our own manner of finding solutions to problems, than in God's.

We have been thinking in this chapter about the resources the Church has to give our common society, not in the first instance by planning or publicity or commissions, but by the power and in the name of Jesus. The Church cannot use any other power without grasping at another kingdom. The Church is not ever an alternative government. We cannot subscribe to the dictum 'Seek ye first the political kingdom and all these things will be added to you'. When the people wanted to make him king, Jesus withdrew himself.

The kingdom is the reign of Jesus Christ. It does not belong to us. When we grasp some kind of a kingdom of our own, we are in effect disinherited, because we cannot produce the fruits of his kingdom. These can only be produced if we are dependent on him as branches depend on a vine. (John 15: vv. 1–11). If we strive for a kingdom with our own specifications, we will certainly have our reward. We may get what we have striven for, whether this is a sacramental system, a charismatic movement, more efficient church government or the political solution to which we are dedicated, but we are likely to find ourselves strangely in a kingdom that is not Christ's.

We may never speak and make decisions as those who

seek their own kingdom. We can do no other than the Lord who said, 'Truly I say to you, the Son can do nothing of his own accord, but only what he sees the Father doing.' (John 5: v. 19). We are to seek in obedience the mind of the living God. Woe to us if we try to possess God's vineyard and use his Church to advance the cause of our own kingdoms.

Let us now and always joyfully let God be God. It may be that as we move towards the twenty-first century, we are entering upon a time of judgement in which many of us will be severely tested. We should not fear that, but we should prepare for it by putting on the whole armour of God. It may well be that the divine initiative in pouring out his Holy Spirit in so many parts of the world in these last days is his preparation of us for what lies ahead.

I remember vividly one of the last speeches made at the Anglican Consultative Council in Trinidad a few years ago. It was made by the Bishop of Singapore. He said something like this: 'Much of our speaking about justice and peace, and about the re-structuring of the Church, presupposes that the Church and its people are free to determine what sort of society they will live in, and what will be the shape of the Church. This sort of debate may be relevant in democratic societies. But Christians in much of the world are no longer able to share in determining the policies of their governments, nor wholly free to determine the shape of the Church. The future in South East Asia is uncertain. What we most urgently need to do is to prepare for a future in which we may find ourselves, for example, living in a society in which freedom of expression does not exist and in which freedom of religion means on the one hand freedom only to worship in a Church but not to propagate the faith, and on the other, freedom for anti-religious propaganda. In such circumstances cultural Christianity will not survive. Only those who experience the love of God in

Jesus as an abiding presence in the Holy Spirit will stand fast. It is to this that we need most urgently to address ourselves.' I believe he is right.

Whether the Church exists in the faltering West, in the Marxist East or in right-wing dictatorships in various parts of the world, Christians will have no effective witness to make unless they are led to appropriate their full inheritance as the sons of God filled and aglow with the Holy Spirit. I praise God very much that wherever one travels in the world one finds evidence that the Lord is renewing his Church. I rejoice in this breath-taking divine initiative, and we can take courage from it for 'whatever is born of God overcomes the world'. (1 John 5: v. 4).

2

The Spirit and evangelism

David Pytches
Former Bishop of Chile, Bolivia and Peru

2

THE MALE EGO CAN BE SERIOUSLY DEFLATED WHEN THE WOMAN GETS there first. Mary did in 1969, and it was an embarrassment to me. She got into the wrong company on the boat travelling back to Chile and emerged with a fresh 'You-know-what' glow about her, speaking in tongues and all that. If only she had been prepared to argue with me about it *first*, I would have been on strong ground, and I would have been able to reason her out of it. But she was much too wise for that, before *and* after her experience. She just began to live a new kind of life. My defences were down, and I was forced to sue for peace. So I decided to seek the same experience myself. About six months later it happened. That which is not always easy to define became solid reality to me. I knew I had been filled with the Holy Spirit. Everything good became delightfully new. The only snag it seemed was that I had just been made a suffragan bishop. The 'safety-first' syndrome took over.

As 'team captain' I obviously had to be careful. It would have been irresponsible to have done otherwise. For one thing, part of my role as bishop meant I had to 'maintain the unity of the Spirit', and not everyone shared the new vision we were receiving. But there are also dangers in being over-cautious and timid. However God has his ways of dealing with even over-cautious bishops, and Mary was again the culprit when she invited Kath to visit us.

Kath was a missionary friend of ours who was working in the Provinces of Malleco and Cautin, where our largest work is. She had been home in England in the mid 60's and came back to Chile joyfully renewed. As is the case the 'infection' spread. When news reached the authorities meeting in Santiago that some of the young men training in the seminary at Maquehue-Pelal, where Kath taught, were allegedly 'filled with the Spirit' and 'speaking in tongues', we were beginning to feel disturbed. Apparently she had been lecturing on the epistles to the Corinthians. Dangerous material in South America. After a discussion on spiritual gifts for the Church today some students asked her to lay hands on them and pray. The reaction to all this from the powers-that-be was quick. 'That it might spread no further' Kath was asked to desist from 'pentecostal' practices and she graciously gave us that assurance. This submission to discipline did not pass unnoticed, though for Kath it was costly. But by then there was no way of stopping things. In her part of Chile the Holy Spirit was truly on the move by the end of the 60's, and renewal spread to missionaries in the North early in 1970.

Kath's arrival was crucial, and her visit happened to coincide with one from a retired missionary from Guatemala who was with us to challenge us about 'activating the laity'. So a meeting was called for the following evening, and we invited as many people as possible from the neighbourhood. We grasped the nettle firmly and asked Kath to speak to us. It all went very well until the end. People began to go forward for prayer and the laying-on of hands. I then found myself conducting a lonely dialogue with the Lord.

The Lord Go forward.
Self   But Lord, I'm the organiser of the meeting,
           and organisers don't go forward and ask for
           prayer like that!

The Lord I'm telling you to go forward.

Self   But Lord, I've already experienced renewal.

The Lord I know all about that, but you have been around here ten years and never told my Church about its resources in the Holy Spirit.

Self   But, Lord, there's a woman up there laying hands on people, and I'm a bishop.

The Lord Stop making excuses. Go on up. It is necessary for you as 'team captain' to publicly identify yourself with what I'm doing.

I obeyed.

Renewal and Church growth

Personal renewal is one thing. An essential. Church growth is another, but the two should be vitally linked. We are grateful to God that in South America the one has led to the other, and it is this that I want to share. But first I need to sketch something of the background of Chile as I know it, and the Church situation as it has so far developed there.

There is a great deal of talk today about evangelism. It was my privilege to work for seventeen years in South America, where evangelism looks easy. It is never easy. But sometimes it looks that way. Neverthless in recent years Church growth has been phenomenal in South America, and I have had the good fortune to observe it at close range.

Most of what I have to say concerns Chile, although for the last five years I was bishop of the Anglican diocese which also includes Bolivia and Peru. Chile has been much in the news in recent years with the Marxist government of the late President Allende and its overthrow in September 1973. The population of the Republic of Chile is around ten million. The Anglican Church is one of many different Churches in the country. It is the oldest Protestant Church in Chile and was the first to be given legal status by the Chilean government, although it is small in size. The Pentecostals are far and away the largest non-Catholic group, divided into as many as eighty legally separate denominations. The Roman Catholic Church claims the nominal allegiance of about 80% of the population, although of that number only 10% attend Mass regularly.

For many years the English settlers did not attempt any evangelism for fear of it being regarded as sheep stealing and thus prejudicing their trading privileges. Worship was commenced in English in the 1820's, although Chileans speak Spanish. But when Allen Gardiner Jr. came to Lota in 1860 he used his position as Chaplain to the English community for pioneer outreach amongst the Araucanian Indians in the Provinces of Malleco and Cautin. In addition, Bible translating was done, medical and educational work undertaken, and industrial and agricultural projects started. There was no great desire to establish an Anglican Church in Chile, although one did slowly emerge, and by the end of the 1940's two Araucanians had been ordained. In 1958 the Spanish-speaking element began to assume an Anglican identity after encouraging statements at the Lambeth Conference. In recent years the Spanish-speaking work has grown particularly in the rural situation in Malleco and Cautin and the urban areas in the capital city of Santiago and the Province of Valparaiso. There has been considerable growth in the period 1960–76. In 1960 there were 31 congregations, 51 in 1970, and 82 in 1976. This is encouraging growth for a small Church, so it is worth seeing how it came about and what were the factors behind it.

Indigenous leadership

Growth has taken place, firstly, because the Chileans themselves have been involved in the work of church-planting. Some of these pioneers have since been ordained. At the time of writing we have one Chilean bishop and 26 national clergy of whom 8 are full time. There is one English bishop and 5 clergy. In using Chileans we have run risks. Inevitably most of these leaders have a limited 'feel' for Anglican traditions, and this is reflected in the new churches which have come into being. But life has to come before order, Spirit before bones. One cannot order a non-existent army. And when the Holy Spirit breathes life into people and brings to birth new churches, the structure and discipline should be adapted to the local culture rather than that of the missionary home-land. We made the mistake for a long time of trying to transplant strict Anglican order into a totally different situation. It was a deadly mistake. Our hesitations were grounded on the fear that the emerging Church would be unrecognisable as Anglican. We needed to be liberated by the Holy Spirit from Old World paternalism before we could press forward with confidence and see the growth that has since followed.

Spiritual resources

Here we need to sketch in the political back-cloth which led us to face up to our spiritual impoverishment. Late in 1971 some church leaders met in Valparaiso to discuss emergency measures in the light of political developments then taking place in Chile. The question we had to answer was 'what will happen if all missionaries are forced to leave Chile?' One of the Chilean clergy brought a stranger to this meeting who turned out to be that retired missionary from

Guatemala mentioned earlier. He said he had two questions he wanted to ask us. First of all, what were we doing to prepare the Church for a Marxist dictatorship? And, secondly, what were we doing to bring the laity out of cold storage and into active leadership?

President Allende had been elected as Chile's first Marxist President in 1970. According to all the propaganda this was to be a uniquely Chilean experiment in Marxism. It was soon apparent that the sweeping restructuring of society outlined in the 'Popular Unity' programme was going to be impossible to achieve democratically, and that to continue in office Allende would have to violate the constitution and establish himself as dictator. We had qualms about the injustices and inequalities of the capitalism we had seen in Chile. But also we had read enough missionary history to know what had happened to the Christian Church in other parts of the world under Marxist regimes. In China, for example, the Marxists had been careful not to attack the Church itself but slowly to undermine the integrity of Church leaders. The possibility of the Church in Chile becoming 'orphaned' appeared to be a real one. Missionaries would have to leave. National leaders in the Church would be arrested. What would happen to the Church? And what were we doing about it?

We had become aware of our failure to prepare the Church adequately. We had training programmes, but text books were limited and some of the books had not even been translated yet. How was the Church going to be taught in a Communist country, and who was going to do it when we had all left? The answer is obvious, though we had missed it in our pride. The Holy Spirit was God's provision for all these needs. He was as alive and active today as at Pentecost and during the equally turbulent days of the

Early Church. We were humbled when we realised what we had missed. We had not taught the Church about the resources of the Holy Spirit, and how they can be received. He was the Counsellor provided for an 'orphaned' Church (John 6: v. 7), the Teacher to guide it into all truth (John 16: v. 13). We had simply to believe in the promises of God. We sought and found, as has already been recounted.

Renewal leads to outreach

Omar was a busy man. For some years he had been combining work for the Bible Society with running a small suburban church in Santiago in his spare time. Although some solid foundations had been laid, this church never really got off the ground. Then the Rev. Omar Ortiz left to take charge of a new church on a housing estate outside Vina del Mar in the Valparaiso area. Omar felt ill-equipped to take on such a responsibility. At the weekly staff meeting he learned that one of the missionary clergy was going to give some Bible teaching in a Roman Catholic retreat. Omar asked what the purpose of the retreat was, and learned that it was for *renovacion* or renewal. Omar thought that if anyone needed 'renovating' he did, and he wondered if they would let him come too. Arrangements were soon made for him to go along with one of his leading church members.

Omar returned from the retreat on top of the world. The 'renovation' had taken place, and his lay friend had had a similar experience. Being 'filled with the Holy Spirit' was a reality for them both and there was a great change in them. So they thought they ought to get their church council together for a time of prayer. It seemed like 'heaven on earth', so they met the next night also. Again, they were blessed. But the third night was a bit of an anti-climax and

they were disappointed. But they then began to realise that
the Spirit of God was going deeper with them, and revealing the things that had to be put right before further blessing would come. They became acutely aware of jealousies
and resentments, criticisms and unloving attitudes, which
they realised had to be put right. God seemed to be saying
to them that it was no good spreading 'good news' before
there was a loving fellowship to receive any new spiritual
babies. It was a humbling experience, but forgiveness and
reconciliation were sought and found.

Then they went back to God in prayer for directions as to
what he wanted them to do next. He showed them that he
wanted them to have a campaign based on their own
church to reach out to the people round about. It was to be
a 'do-it-yourself' effort and no outside evangelist was to be
invited. Once the meetings began there was no stopping
them. Only the mid-night curfew forced the meetings to
stop. From seven in the morning onwards Omar was
beseiged with people at his house wanting counselling for
all sorts of things.

After about ten days of this he came to see me. I could
see that he was worn out and so I sent him South for two
weeks' rest. When he returned the meetings were still
going on and lasted for another two months. Many people
came to the Lord. Time was to prove that not all the
conversions were genuine. As in the parable of the sower
there were disappointments, but there was also a good
harvest. In describing these wonderful months Omar
said:

'I had often read in the Acts of the Apostles about the
Lord "adding daily to the Church", but I always had a
sneaking feeling that a little bit of exaggeration had crept
into the text at that point. But now I have seen it for
myself.'

A few months later he asked for help at a mass baptism which he had arranged at the river-side. There were over a hundred candidates, and we had them in three lines at the river's edge, one for total immersion, another for the 'up-to-the-knees-in-water-and-sprinkling' variety, and the third for standing on dry land and sprinkling, all to show the comprehensiveness of the Anglican Church! Afterwards we gathered on the green grass beside the river and had a great time of praise and worship, many dancing with joy before the Lord. It seemed a perfectly normal thing to do.

I wanted to check up a bit myself, so I singled out a young man called Juan Carlos. I found his understanding of the Christian Faith satisfactory. I then asked him to say what real difference it had made to him becoming a Christian. His face dropped! 'Can't you *see*?' he replied.

'Well I can see that you are obviously happy,' I said, 'but then I did not know you before. Can you give me an instance of something to convince me that it isn't mere emotionalism.'

He thought for a moment and then confided, 'I can talk to my father now. For four years we have not been communicating though we lived in the same house.'

I asked several others and received equally satisfying replies. Juan Carlos has been a guest speaker for three years running at an annual national conference of school social workers. The other speakers have been educationalists, psychologists and sociologists of high repute. But the half hour slot given to Juan Carlos has been reported as one of the most valuable contributions. Social workers are often at their wits-end trying to help drug addicts. Each year Juan Carlos has humbly shared with these 'experts' how he found liberation from his own drug problem through the power of Jesus Christ in the Church.

Spiritual gifts and evangelism

The next story comes from a rural area in the south of
central Chile. One of our more long-standing rural
churches is located at a place called Petraco about eight
miles from Chol Chol. The congregation was small and
faithful but not very lively. There were between 25 and 30
members. One of the church families had a sad problem. A
woman in their household would periodically go beserk
and take a knife or a chopper to the persons nearest to her
and try to kill them. The family had to watch her round-
the-clock. When the problem became too much for them
some of the local church joined a rota for watching her. But
the problem dragged on. The strain was telling on everyone
and at last the local pastor went to the minister of the
mother church at Chol Chol. He discussed it with the Rev.
José Angel Cabezas in charge of the zone, who promised to
come out the following Sunday to see what the Lord would
have them do. For over 10 years in Chol Chol they had
been praying daily that the Lord would manifest his power
and glory but so far their prayers had not apparently been
answered. When José arrived at the little church at Petraco
with its mud floor and tin roof he called for the poor
demented creature to be brought forward. After prayer he
felt led by the Spirit of God to exorcise an evil spirit in her.
The woman immediately collapsed on the floor. They
thought she was dead. After two or three very puzzling
minutes the body rose up from the floor and raised her
arms to the roof and began to give glory to God. The whole
church burst into praise. The news spread round the whole
region like wildfire and folk in that animistic culture began
to turn to Christ. Some five new churches soon sprang into
being round about, each of them as big numerically as the
original church of Petraco. It was my privilege to visit the

area some months later and I was able to meet representatives from these five new congregations all gathered into one of their newly built churches. We had a great day of worship with marriages, baptisms, confirmations, praise, testimonies, teaching and singing. At one point the ranks parted and a Mapuche woman came to the front. There was a solemn hush and it was clear that she was held in high esteem by the brethren. She began to prophesy. She knew little of the Bible but all she said was in accord with the Word of God and she challenged the brethren in God's name to keep their worship free from anything pertaining to their former animism and to remember that the Church was a virgin to be kept pure and ready as a bride for the coming of Christ the Bridegroom. I stood by in surprise. I had not realised that we had prophetesses in the Anglican Church. But then these people were hardly aware that they were Anglicans! We broke off for an informal picnic lunch before returning inside for fellowship together, and in a final act of worship partaking in the Holy Communion. If their knowledge of the Bible was limited their knowledge of the Prayer Book was nil. It fell to my lot to lead the Eucharist. I selected portions of the liturgy sparingly and mainly the parts I knew off by heart in Spanish. I remember we were coming up to the Sanctus 'Therefore with angels and archangels, and with all the company of heaven, we laud and magnify thy glorious name, ever more praising thee and saying . . .' Suddenly the congregation was up on its feet. Arms were stretched out to heaven and the whole company were praising God with full voice. I was caught unawares. 'This isn't in the Prayer Book rubrics,' I thought to myself. But it was wonderful to be in the middle of it all. Was this a violation of St. Paul's 'decently and in order' clause of 1 Cor. 14: 40, I wondered? I reassured myself that in fact it wasn't because I was sure that if I had called them to stop they would have done so. But I had no wish to do it. In fact as the praise continued ascending so spontaneously I realised that it was perfectly in order both in the spirit of our worship and in the letter of the law. Had not our liturgy directed them 'to laud and magnify his glorious name in the company of all the hosts of heaven'? Who was I to stop them when they were doing so admirably what I had just told them to do? I do not remember how long the general adoration continued but it seemed appropriate to let it roll. The Lord was truly exalted and present in our midst . . . 'enthroned on the praises of Israel' (Ps. 22:3). This was the real presence!

It was a lesson and challenge to me. The devotion of these folk from the rural areas of Araucania where their animistic culture still prevailed ought not to have surprised me as it did. They seemed to love God so much more than I did. One was forced to realise the relevance of the gospel to them. They had known a darkness I had never known and had been brought out of this darkness into the marvellous light of the gospel of Jesus. They had been brought up all their life subject to fear. And only those who have lived in a culture where spirits are worshipped can understand such fear. They had imagined that this was their lot for life and that there was no way out. Then they had found liberation through Jesus. In him they discovered the perfect love which casts out fear.

* * *

This simple and selected account of the way the Spirit of God has been moving must inevitably accept the limits of time and space. My colleagues in Chile could describe similar experiences which they have witnessed. In conclusion however there are a few general observations which appear to be worth making.

1   It is clear from the Acts of the Apostles that evangelism is a normal outworking of a movement of God's Spirit. We began to discover that this was happening throughout our work in Chile and yet we had given very little teaching on evangelism itself. We had never had a conference or a commission on evangelism as far as I can remember.

2   Renewal in the Spirit brings a greater reality to worship. This in itself is evangelistic. Christians enjoy their worship so much that they begin to persuade friends to come to church. There, through the work of the Holy Spirit, the outsider finds (as in 1 Cor. 14: 25) that 'the secrets of his heart are disclosed and so falling down on his face he will worship God and declare that God is really among you.' This was the experience in the congregation on the housing estate mentioned in the Valparaiso region.

3   Renewal in the Spirit brings a greater sense of expectancy. Manifestations of power through miracles of healing or exorcism are occasions for evangelism. It certainly gives people something to talk about and the Christian can use the opportunity to share his own belief. The example of the happenings in the rural area around Petraco is a case in point.

4   Renewal in the Spirit means that the Church is made aware of the differing gifts of the Spirit which God has given to his Church and the gift of evangelism will be rediscovered and given its rightful emphasis.

5   Renewal in the Spirit means that leaders who have experienced it can trust the Holy Spirit in others to do the Lord's work through them even if it isn't quite the way one had expected it would be done. There will also be mistakes but these are occasions for learning, sharing and teaching. Delegation, love and trust are essential in Church growth.

The wind of the Spirit is blowing in Chile. As in many

other parts of the world we see a moving and a growing Church there. Many problems, difficulties and disappointments confront the Church. There is much work still to be done. But we can go forward trusting the same Spirit to give the counsel, wisdom, guidance and grace to help the Church to go on to maturity.

*   *   *

3

The Spirit and community

William Frey
Bishop of Colorado, U.S.A.

3

WHEN MY FIVE CHILDREN WERE YOUNGER, I USED TO WONDER HOW I MIGHT BEST convince them of their father's love. I thought of many schemes and concocted several fantasies. In one, I imagined that I would parade them all in the living room, seat myself in a large chair in the middle, and say something like this: 'My children, I have something very important to say to you and I don't want you ever to forget it. But listen very carefully, because I'm only going to say it once. Your father loves you very, very much. Now you may go, but in any time of pain or distress, difficulties or loneliness, just remember what I have said and you will be comforted.'

Obviously that was not very satisfactory so I thought of another scheme. I would write each of them a letter saying, 'Dear Paul, Mark, Matthew, Peter, or Susy, your father loves you very much. Please carry this with you at all times, and if you ever need comfort or help, take it from your pocket and read it and you will be strengthened. Love and kisses, Daddy.'

An improvement to be sure, but it still lacked the essential ingredient that we have all come to know and to cherish. That ingredient is, of course, the personal presence and warmth of human touch. For when a child comes running into the house crying because of a bruised knee or a battered ego, a memory, however vivid, and words, however well intentioned, are inadequate. What is needed is the tenderness and warmth of a human embrace. The child must be gathered up into one's arms to know the comfort which comes only as body touches body. Love must be expressed in physical form.

Divine love, like human love, must be expressed in physical form too, if it is to do what it is meant to do. The analogy is imperfect of course, but it may serve. It is helpful to know that 'God loved the world so much that he gave his only begotten Son.' But that happened long ago, before you or I ever saw the light of day. And it is helpful to have a written record of those mighty acts by which we have been redeemed. It is good to have the Lord's love letters to his children, the Scriptures. But what is needed, in addition to all of this, is the *incarnate* love of God. The word of life must take flesh in our day if the world is to know God's love in all its fullness. That is what the Christian community is all about.

The Christian community, the Church, is not meant to be simply a vehicle for preaching the Gospel of Jesus Christ, nor is it to be merely a society organised to accomplish some of those projects which the Gospel envisions. In a very deep sense the Church is meant to be an integral part of the Gospel proclamation. It is part of what Jesus has promised, and part of what he gives to those who respond to his love.

To put it another way, the Christian community is meant to be a body that can make the comfortable words its own, 'Come unto *us* all ye that travail and are heavy laden.'

One of our contemporary theologians (J.J. Von Allmen) put it like this: 'A baptised person is a sign of promise for all men. The Eucharist is a promise for every meal. The Church is a promise for all human society.' To paraphrase a German theologian, the Church is to be the *'prolepsis* of the *eschatōn'*, a phrase which might be rendered 'that society or community where the promises and the power of the risen Christ are already at work in some measurable degree, a foretaste of good things yet to come.' Or as they say at the movies, 'the preview of coming attractions'.

These are bold statements, and in making them one is immediately struck by the enormous chasm which separates the Church that ought to be (the Church which the Lord is preparing as his Bride 'without spot or wrinkle') and the Church as most of us experience it on a day-to-day basis. Most of our theological assertions about the Christian Church sound like interesting but ultimately meaningless abstractions when compared with what most of us see in our local parish.

The Holy Spirit alone can bring together our theory and our practice. I am convinced that the most important aspect of the current movement of the Spirit, and the one which will have the most far-reaching effects on the Church and the world, is the renewal in our midst of the concept and the practice of true Christian community, what the New Testament calls *koinōnia*. As Paul put it, 'the creation waits with eager longing for the revealing of the Sons of God.' (Romans 8: v. 19) In other words, the whole universe is waiting for us to get our act together.

What follows will be largely autobiographical, experiential rather than philosophical. I make no apologies for this, since it is my understanding that most good theology is historical rather than theoretical. We begin with the experience of something that God does in history, and then proceed prayerfully to draw certain conclusions from it. This reflection upon God's activity is what we call theology. For example, Jewish theology is basically a reflection on the Exodus. 'We were Pharaoh's slaves in Egypt; and the Lord brought us out of Egypt with a mighty hand.'

(Deuteronomy 6: v. 21) Christian theology is largely experiential too: 'One thing I know, that though I was blind, now I see.' (John 9: v. 25), 'Can anyone forbid water for baptising these people who have received the Holy Spirit just as we have?' (Acts 10: v. 47) And it all begins with the Resurrection: 'This Jesus . . . you crucified and killed . . . but God raised him up.' (Acts 2: vv. 23, 24)

To speak of one's experience is a dangerous thing. Self deception is a trap into which we can easily fall. Hence, what follows must be thought of as descriptive rather than prescriptive. It may have some value, however, for learning how God deals with a family may offer some clues at least to how he deals with the Church.

In 1971 I had been Bishop of the small Diocese of Guatemala for almost four years. We had struggled in those days with a number of seemingly unrelated issues. We searched for ways to relate the Gospel to an oppressive political climate, where violence and injustice of every sort appeared to be woven into the fabric of society. We tried to help individual Christians to stand firm in the midst of such a situation. We asked ourselves how the Church could sink deep roots into the soil of a country where for years our principal leaders had been foreign missionaries, how to develop effective leadership without unconsciously producing carbon copies of foreign patterns. We even struggled with the problem, perhaps peculiar to Episcopalians, of how to maintain our tradition of liturgical participation in a place where the illiteracy rate was 80% and where consequently a Prayer Book was virtually useless. We found a few clues to these problems, but were usually dissatisfied with most of our results. Our theory and our practice always seemed to be far apart.

Our home had become something like a hotel. We had a constant stream of visitors. Clergy and their families from the rural missions, visiting dignitaries from the United States and other countries, all became part of our family life. We made provisions for our 'extended family' early on, by adding a couple of guest rooms at the rear of the bishop's residence. In one sense this was excellent preparation for what God had in store for the future; but in another it was not. We generally kept our guests at arm's length from our own life. And they were treated as guests – welcome guests to be sure – but not members of the family.

My personal life as bishop was marked by some startling contrasts. On the outside there was undoubtedly the image of a successful cleric. But the outer facade rarely matched the inner reality.

For example, intellectually and emotionally, I was committed to social justice and political change, but unable to change my own lifestyle enough so that it would adequately reflect the sort of values which I proclaimed. I talked a lot about the family as the basic unit in the Christian Church, but I neglected my own family. I always did it for the finest reasons of course – jobs to be finished, trips to be made, counselling to be done. But neglect, however well intentioned, brings its inevitable harvest. I was haunted by those verses in Paul's letter to Timothy where he speaks about a bishop needing to be able to manage his own household. There was a recurrent fantasy nightmare in which I would imagine myself preaching a fine sermon on Christian love and responsibility, when suddenly my wife or one of my children would stand up in the midst of the congregation, and reveal the reality of my own failures.

Two of our teenagers became involved in the use of drugs, one of them so deeply that he was a virtual stranger under our roof, isolated from us and from everyone else by invisible walls which no one could penetrate.

At the root of all of this was undoubtedly a failure in spirituality. I talked a lot about the value and the nature of prayer, but in reality I prayed very little.

There were externally caused tensions as well. Because of my attempts to let the Christian Church become a meeting ground for the warring political factions in Guatemala, the military government then in power came to suspect me of subversive activity. These suspicions resulted in subtle harassment, surveillance, and telephone taps. The strains from within and from without took their toll. I began to find it difficult to sleep at nights without a sleeping pill or two, washed down by large quantities of alcohol. Before I knew it I was chemically dependent without even knowing the terminology.

This of course added an additional complication to relationships within the family. The children knew of my consumption of alcohol, and therefore paid little heed to my warnings about drugs. I suspect that it was only God's grace and my own fear which saved me from a number of other potential moral lapses. Just as the quest for personal holiness can sometimes blind a person to the need for social justice, so the quest for social justice can often blind one to the need for personal holiness. And the silent acceptance of moral erosion in myself and others was a reflection of great spiritual deterioration.

I was troubled by the fact that my children were not growing up as Christians. (I had not yet heard David du Plessis' lovely maxim, 'God has no grandchildren'.) I had the same arguments with my children that other people have with theirs. It struck me with appalling force one Sunday morning when debating with one of my more rebellious teenage sons about the merits of church attendance. He baulked, and I finally played my trump card. I said, 'What's the matter? Don't you love God any more?' His reply was quick and revealing: 'Sure I love God, Dad, I just hate church.'

Oddly enough that was the straw that broke the camel's back. On Ash Wednesday, almost out of desperation, I announced a Lenten Bible study to be conducted around the dining room table immediately following the evening meal. The announcement, predictably, was met with something less than great enthusiasm. But with all of the strength that I could muster I imposed my will and we began.

We read the Gospel of Mark, probably because it is the shortest. I don't remember a great deal about the study except for one evening when we came across that passage in the sixth chapter where Mark tells of Jesus' return to his home town. Verse five suddenly came across with new meaning. 'And he could do no mighty work there, except that he laid his hands upon a few sick people and healed them . . . and he marvelled because of their unbelief.'

Two things immediately leapt out at me. First of all, it was appallingly evident why Jesus was unable to do any mighty work in his own home town. The people had become too familiar with him. They thought they knew him, but didn't. They could not see the great change that had come about since he left to begin his public ministry. 'That's just old Jesus,' the people must have said. 'We've known him for years. Nothing special about him.' I thought of my own life as a cleric, in which the things of God can all too easily become little more than the tools of one's trade; how easy it is to let familiarity with holy things blind one to their awesome power and majesty. How simple to believe that one knows and understands such things as the Scriptures, the Eucharist, and prayer simply because one is exposed to them on a regular basis. How easy it is for a professional to slip into an impersonal professionalism, and even to justify the hasty handling of the numinous on the grounds of administrative efficiency. How easy to let one's routine become routine.

But the second thing hit me with even greater force. 'He could do no mighty work.' Yet he healed some people. I was amazed at Mark's expectations. They were light years beyond mine. I thought the healing of the sick through the laying on of hands was a mighty thing indeed. When Mark spoke of that as something almost beneath his notice, I wondered what he was expecting. And I began to interpret in theological terms something with which I dealt with routinely in the political realm, the 'revolution of rising expectations.'

A revolution of rising expectations is what happens when a person who is poor, and doesn't know he's poor because he has no one else to compare himself with except other poor people, suddenly discovers that poverty is not inevitable. He finds that some people are wealthy, that some people are not condemned to live out their lives in want and misery. His expectations begin to rise. Seeing that more is available, he begins to expect more; expecting more he begins to demand more. If enough people do this together, they exert upward pressure on the political structure, and revolutionary changes take place. Sometimes they come about peacefully, sometimes violently, but they are changes. 'The Kingdom of Heaven has been coming violently and men of violence take it by force.' (Matthew 11: v. 12) The one who expects more gets more.

It occurred to me that one of the reasons I had been receiving so little of the grace of God was that I was expecting so little. Expecting little, I sought little. There had even been times *when I thought* we *ought* to expect little, times when I wanted to canonise my own spiritual dryness. My difficulty came from an unexamined area of

unbelief deep in my own heart. I was now beginning to see
that God often delays answering some of our prayers until
they reflect a deep desire and longing within, prayers of the
heart. So I began my own private and quiet revolution of
rising expectations, expecting God to manifest himself
today with the same power with which he had manifested
himself in centuries past.

Late in 1971 my family and I were expelled from
Guatemala. My efforts to exert some Christian influence to
bring about a diminution of the torture and bloodshed
which characterised political life there had apparently
caused consternation in government circles. Public accusations were made, and I was labelled as a Communist agent,
a political meddler, and a subversive.

The accusations, of course, hurt. Worse was the fact that
some of our friends believed the propaganda. And the
forced separation from people we had come to know and to
love was painful beyond description. However, a strange
thing happened. I found that I could feel no hatred or
hostility towards those responsible. There was dismay,
sadness and tears, but no anger. I found that I could pray
for them with an honest heart. This was, for me at least, a
minor miracle, since I did not naturally react in that way
toward those who frustrate my schemes and accuse me
unjustly. I assumed that it must be the Holy Spirit doing
something within me which I was unable to do by myself.

At the same time our whole family had a sense of being
engulfed by the power and the love of God, as though we
were being supported by unseen hands, and we were able
to make our hasty preparations for departure with relative
tranquility, and with a deep inner awareness of Christ's
victory. Again, I attributed this to the activity of the Holy
Spirit, and to a fulfilment of the Lord's promise of blessing
on those who are persecuted for the sake of justice. But I

was amazed by the power of it all. I thought such blessings were reserved for some future time, and I was unprepared for the force of it in the present.

The spiritual euphoria lasted for days. The pain of being wrenched from our home and our loved ones was acute, but it was accompanied by something even deeper than suffering, something which put the pain into a different perspective. We had the feeling of having reached the bottom only to discover that the bottom was very solid and supportive.

As might be expected in the case of an exiled bishop, there was a fair amount of publicity surrounding our departure. I received numerous requests to speak to Church groups around the country. People generally expected a talk on the cost of discipleship, the conflict between Christ and modern Caesars, with references to CIA involvement in Latin America. When I was asked if the conflict was political or theological, my immediate response was to say that it was theological since it involved the struggle between the sovereignty of Jesus Christ and the sovereignty of the earthly powers. Upon reflection I came to see that it was both, because it took place in that ambiguous area where theology and politics overlap, a fact too often forgotten by exponents of a purely 'spiritual' gospel. 'Jesus is Lord' is a radical theological *and* political statement. For it means that Jesus is Lord of all life, not simply what we have come to call our religious life.

As I travelled and spoke I found that I could easily expound on all of the desired topics. But inwardly I was still reeling because of the effects of what I was learning. And toward the end of all my talks, after trotting out my litany of horrors, relating the almost incredible instances of repression, torture, mass murder and all of the rest, I would change the subject and say something like 'all of this is very interesting and very important, but what I really want you to know is that the Gospel promises are true. God really does uphold and sustain those who are persecuted for the sake of the Gospel, and his presence and power and love are as available today as they were in the days of the early Christian persecutions.' It is some sort of commentary on the general state of the Church in those days that the more I talked about this, the quicker the audiences lost interest, and the fewer invitations I received.

Exiled bishops can be something of an embarrassment, but through the extreme kindness and generosity of the Bishop of Arkansas, I was offered a job as University Chaplain in Fayetteville, coupled with a curacy in the local parish, St. Paul's. We were warmly welcomed and received into that Christian community. And it was there that we came face to face with what has come to be known as the Charismatic Renewal.

Over the years I had occasionally run across people who identified themselves as 'charismatic Christians' (a phrase by the way, which I consider to be redundant.) Some appeared to be neurotic and pushy. Others spoke of the Holy Spirit in terms which I thought I already understood. So my reaction to them was mixed. If their 'baptism in the Spirit' was what made them neurotic, I didn't want it. On the other hand, if they were simply excited about things I already knew, I didn't need it.

There were a few exceptions to the above, a few whose new life in the Spirit had given them an authentic inner peace, an enviable joy, and a remarkable ability to love and serve others in the power of Christ. So when a prayer group was formed at St. Paul's, led by a known charismatic, I began to attend, taking with me a strange mixture of curiosity, apprehension, and imagined spiritual superiority. In one sense I was anxious to go. I had heard that such groups invariably manifested every conceivable ecclesiastical sin. They were fundamentalistic and anti-intellectual, holier-than-thou and theologically confused, they were disruptive and divisive; and worst of all, they were often anti-clerical! I would go to set them straight.

In one sense I was disappointed. There were no obvious neurotics, simply a group of rather average Episcopalians who were in the initial stages of their own revolution of rising expectations and who were beginning to fall in love with Jesus Christ. As we prayed together, one person prayed in tongues. There were no histrionics, no rolling on the floor, no frothing at the mouth. She simply switched languages as easily as I might have begun to pray in Spanish. My reaction, or lack of one, surprised me. And as we continued to pray, I sensed a recurrence of the same sort of an awareness of God's overwhelming and loving presence that we had known during our last days in Guatemala.

The authentic experience of God's presence comes on a level far deeper than that of the emotions. One's emotions are not absent from the experience, but they are not the source of it, nor are they reliable indicators of its reality and intensity. One senses the presence of God in much the same way that one experiences a full stomach after a hearty meal. It is more a matter of *knowing* than feeling. 'In that day you will know that I am in my father, and you in me, and I in you.' (John 14:20) Whatever emotion emerges is a response to the knowledge.

That night I knew something with an intensity which by comparison made my previous faith and belief seem like mere suspicion. And there was an almost involuntary inner response to the knowledge. I was overcome with a desire, or rather a need to pray. All sorts of prayer, day and night. This was accompanied by a deep hunger for the Bible. I couldn't put the Bible down, and I soaked it up like a thirsty desert after a downpour.

As I eagerly devoured the New Testament again, I noticed that it was like a new book. It was as though all previous readings had been done with a veil over my eyes. Passages which once I had overlooked, or dismissed because I couldn't understand them, sounded like exciting descriptions of my own experience. A friend had once described a particular theologian as a man who had an almost erotic relationship with the Bible. I began to understand what he meant.

Being a convinced Catholic and sacramental churchman, I encouraged our prayer group to be eucharistically oriented. Previous conflicts about the nature and importance of the Eucharist were exposed as trivial. The real presence of Christ became another of our shared experiences, as Jesus constantly made himself known to us in the breaking of the bread. (Remarkable too was the case of a visiting Pentecostal pastor who came to the same conclusions about the sacrament, in spite of the fact that for years he had preached what might be called 'the real absence'.

I soon noticed changes in other areas of my life. My wife quickly sensed that something was happening. After a few weeks of scepticism and fear she joined me at the prayer group. Similar things began to happen in her life, and as our relationship with Christ intensified, so did our relationship with one another. What had been a good marriage became an outstanding one.

One evening as I was pouring my usual nightcap I discovered much to my surprise that I no longer wanted or needed it. It felt as though I had become allergic to it, and I slept better than I had in years. The next morning a similar thing happened with my pipe, a compulsive companion of some twenty years. At the same time I began to discover that I had been set free from a couple of other internal and external sins of a compulsive nature, sins which I had long despaired of conquering, and with which I had made an uneasy truce. By 'set free' I simply mean that the compulsion was no longer there. In some cases, a new understanding of what was involved destroyed even the temptation. In others, the temptation remained, but I was free *not* to capitulate. It was as though something or someone who had a stranglehold on several departments of my life had suddenly departed.

I came to understand the nature of grace in a new way. It became more a tangible reality than an elusive abstraction. Something that Thomas Merton said many years ago began to make sense; 'Jesus not only *teaches* us the Christian life, he creates it in our souls by the action of his Spirit . . . It is an entirely new spiritual reality, an inner transformation.'

The children watched with nervous apprehension a disruption in what had been a normal pattern of relationships within the home. Change, even for the better, can be upsetting. They wondered why we came home from late night prayer meetings elated rather than exhausted. Then, one by one, they accompanied us, and the process began in them. The older two were released from their dependence on drugs. Our prodigal who had been dead was made alive again. Our home life was being made new, and there was greater joy and peace than ever before, a deeper level of trust and love, and a greater expectancy about God's power to deal effectively with the problems which all families face. And I was discovering afresh that one's ministry is not limited to verbal persuasion and the clever manipulation of words. Where the words come to an end, there is yet a gift to be given. 'For the Kingdom of God does not consist in talk but in power.' (1 Corinthians 4: v. 20)

It was liberating to discover that the Spirit could be trusted to distribute his gifts to all the members of the body, not simply the clergy. I saw people from the prayer group minister effectively in areas of counselling and healing, personal evangelism and teaching, visiting the sick, and in listening to what the Lord is saying to the Church. In all of this I could see in microcosm many of those things which I had always hoped and prayed the Church would be. Consequently I was increasingly puzzled by the fact that the prayer group remained largely on the periphery of the parish's life. Instead of being seen as a fulfilment of hopes and dreams, our activity was viewed by many as a threat, and by others as a curiosity to be endured because the bishop was involved. To be sure, many individuals were having their personal and their family lives transformed, but there was little visible effect on the larger body.

In retrospect, some of this was inevitable. We were very enthusiastic, and many Episcopalians are suspicious of enthusiasm. Undoubtedly it *is* subject to abuse. But lack of it is dangerous too, and in the end can be fatal. Emerson has rightly remarked that 'every great and commanding movement in the annals of the world is the triumph of enthusiasm. Nothing great was ever accomplished without it.' Then too, there was an element of unfamiliarity which distressed some. We came into close contact with people whose whole religious culture – their piety, music, vocabulary, and expression – was foreign to our own. I confess that I often had trouble dealing with this aspect myself. I was a bit nervous about the Pentecostal pyrotechnics which occasionally ignored Paul's advice about decency and order. And on another level, I grew concerned about the vast amounts of apparent spiritual energy which were generated, but which seemed to be hoarded by individuals and never put to work in the service of the larger community.

But in spite of the strangeness, and in spite of the occasional excesses, there was undeniable joy, love, and power. And I could not understand why the larger Church body declined to come to the wedding banquet.

In 1972 when I was elected Bishop of Colorado, I brought to that task a very different orientation from the one I had taken to Guatemala five years earlier. There were still unresolved questions about some of the directions that the renewal seemed to be taking, but I was enthusiastic about sharing the Lord's obvious power to deal effectively with each individual who will let himself be made new. When I laid hands on confirmees, I expected their *lives* to be changed, not simply their religious habits. I was excited about the Gospel, and all that it promises.

A major turning point came in the summer of 1973. While on vacation at the Texas coast, our family spent a week at the Church of the Redeemer in Houston, and lived in one of their extended family households. Much has been written about that parish which need not be repeated here. Suffice it to say that we found there the answers to many of our questions. There was nothing peripheral about the new life at Redeemer. It was woven through the fabric of the parish, and touched young and old alike. It found expression in a closely knit community, where *koinōnia* was a living reality, not just a theological concept. It seemed to begin at the centre, and spread outwards. The energy generated by the Spirit was harnessed to the whole structure, and moved it forward with a powerful but tranquil determination.

My theories, new and old, about the Body of Christ, suddenly came together and I felt much as a paleontologist might feel, who after years of piecing together a few prehistoric bones, is suddenly confronted with a real live dinosaur. We were blessed beyond measure by an experience of being immersed once again in God's love, this time in the flesh and blood of our fellow Christians. At the end of the week it would not do simply to raise my eyes heavenward and say a prayer of thanksgiving. To be consistent with what I was learning, I also had to look the congregation in the eye and say, 'thank you, Jesus.'

Within a month of our return home, the Lord began dropping people on our doorstep and asking us to take them in, this time not as guests, as we had done in Guatemala, but as members of our family so that we could share a common life together. We were involved in a new expression of Christian community before we knew it.

The initial months were difficult and we made many mistakes. By hindsight we probably learned more from these than from our few successes. The first thing we found was the need for authentic openness. We could not afford to remain strangers to one another, still less landlord and tenants, hosts and guests. We had to leave our masks at the door.

Differences in temperament quickly surfaced, and each of us had a number of previously undiscovered areas of sin exposed. We quickly learned that this is part of the process. The Lord must expose and destroy those parts of our nature which are inconsistent with his building plans.

As we learned, we began to grow in numbers as well as in depth. At the time this was written some forty to forty-five people were involved, nineteen in our household, and another twenty to twenty-five in neighbouring homes. We worship together, study scripture together, and share in a ministry together. One of the most obvious effects of all of this is our economy of time, money and human resources. Under the normal patterns of our society, the people in our household would probably be living in five or six separate units. By becoming one, a tremendous amount of unnecessary duplication is avoided; money and time are made available for doing the Lord's work inside and outside the household.

I find that I have more time and energy to do those things that I was commissioned to do. For example, Paul says that a bishop must be given to hospitality. What that generally means however, is that a bishop's *wife* must be given to it. And what of hospitality itself? Surely it means an authentic opening of one's household to others, not simply entertaining. We find that whatever the meaning, there are more hands to do the work. Whether we have a large group in for dinner, or a priest and his family in for a week of rest, recreation, and counselling, the ministry is shared by many people. I have also discovered that I am free to spend more time with other people. And the time itself seems to be more productive than ever before. Living in a body of people who love you enough to tell you the truth about yourself, and who are given to prayer and support, eases to an incredible degree the burdens of the episcopal office.

The archaic episcopal 'we' has taken on a new meaning, as I find that in a very real sense I am becoming a corporate person. My wife and others from our community frequently accompany me on missions and visitations, and sometimes share in the ministry of teaching and worship. It is good to know that I am much less important than I used to imagine myself to be! When someone needs the Bishop, and the Bishop is attending to a previous demand, there are other people immediately available to exercise ministries of presence, of listening, caring, counselling, praying, and serving.

While there are no written rules, it is assumed that what used to be 'mine' is now 'ours'. And those of us who receive salaries simply put them into a common banking account for our corporate tithes and expenses. The compulsive acquisitiveness, characteristic of American culture, is beginning to disappear. We have a long way to go, but a simpler lifestyle is possible. Things matter very little and people matter a great deal.

Although there is no single blueprint for successful Christian community, nor any foolproof model to be copied, there are a few factors that are common to all. The first might be called the incarnational principle, coming to grips with the fact that 'Jesus Christ has come in the flesh' (1 John 4: v. 2). This means committing ourselves to the Body of Christ as we would to the Lord himself. Social scientists have discovered that a person can successfully share his life deeply with a very limited number of people. Jesus shared his with twelve. Our commitment to him must be acted out through our commitment to a specific group of people. The seed must fall into the ground and die if it is to bring forth any fruit. Where we are rootless, we will be fruitless.

The second constant can be labelled the paradox of *koinōnia*. The quest for community will always fail, because community is not built by love of community, but by love of the brethren. *Koinōnia* is almost a by-product of the Spirit's activity as he produces that sort of love in our hearts. Those who love community more than people will destroy community, for people cannot successfully be used as a means. 'We know that we have passed out of death into life, because we love the brethren . . . By this we know love, that he laid down his life for us; and we ought to lay down our lives for the brethren.' (1 John 3: vv. 14, 16)

Still another constant might be summarised as, 'life through death; death through obedience'. Obedience to Jesus Christ and submission to his designs is essential. Bonhoeffer noted years ago that 'whenever Christ calls a man, he bids him come and die'. Participation in the Christian community is a response to that call, for it means a sacrifice of one's self, one's needs, wants, and desires, in order that something new and more glorious might be born. 'Whoever would save his life will lose it; and whoever loses his life for my sake, he will save it.' (Luke 9: v. 24) Paradoxically, the greatest freedom and the greatest joy in the Body of Christ come from our practice of obedience.

There are critics of a closely knit Christian community who feel that such gatherings of Christians means a retreat from the world. Undoubtedly it can be in some specific cases, but in the long run, a deep expression of Christian community is the only way that the Church can be effectively involved in the world. There is no competition between the Church and the world either for our commitment or for God's love. The awesome fact is that God has chosen to love the world *through* the Church. She is meant to be God's vessel of social transformation, and even now, a working model, imperfect to be sure, of the new humanity which God is creating, where 'the blind receive their sight and the lame walk, lepers are cleansed, and the deaf hear, and the dead are raised up, and the poor have good news preached to them.' (Matthew 11: v. 5) It is simply a matter of breaking the old pattern in which individuals live in the world, and go to church, by making it possible for them to live in the Church and go to the world. It was the strength of such a corporate structure which enabled the Apostles to bear witness to the Resurrection with such great power, and which enabled the poor to be cared for, the sick to be healed, and the hungry to be fed. Too often the life of the Church is characterised by fluctuating and fleeting enthusiasms. *Koinōnia* provides the staying power for the long haul.

'The fellowship of the Holy Spirit' is a reference to what happens when the Holy Spirit touches individual people, floods their hearts with the love of Jesus Christ, and through this shared love moulds them into a new society. It is what Jesus meant when he said that 'when two or three are *gathered together* in my Name, there I will be in the midst of them'. We have neglected this sort of *koinōnia*, at least partially because of the subtle seduction of our Western culture with its highly prized individualism. Even those parts of the Christian Church which have laid great emphasis on the necessity of a new birth have often forgotten that birth never takes place in a vacuum. Birth presupposes a family, and the new birth presupposes a new family as visible and as palpable as the one into which we were born 'by the will of man and the will of the flesh'.

When this is forgotten, we do strange things, because the outward machinery of the Church continues to function unchecked. In baptism, for example, we are, among many other things, welcoming people into the Christian family. But in most people's experience the invitation is, 'come, be part of our family, but be quick about it. This family only meets together an hour and a half once a week. The rest of the time you are on your own.' The Body of Christ as often as not can be seen only spasmodically, and then for a brief period of time. It materialises, as by some magician's trick (with a puff of smoke if one is thus inclined liturgically) at 9:00 or 11:00 o'clock on a Sunday morning, and it disappears just as rapidly by noon.

The same sort of thing happens in Christian marriage. The blessing of the Church which two people seek when they come to be married turns out to be a verbal pronouncement by the parish priest, rather than a commitment of the members of the Body to support and uphold the couple as they enter into that volatile and sacramental union. What people ought to be able to expect at such times is the acquisition of a vast multitude of surrogate fathers, mothers, brothers, sisters, aunts, uncles, and cousins. But what they generally receive is merely a pleasant ceremony. It must be said parenthetically that one of the major contributing factors to the near death of marriage in the Western world is the Church's failure to be what it is meant to be, a support community for all of its members, new and old.

There can be then no renewal of the Church which does not involve a profound renewal of *koinōnia*. Martin Buber saw this when he said, 'We are waiting for a theophany (a manifestation of God's presence) about which we know only its location, and that location is community.'

'It was there from the beginning; we have seen it with our own eyes; we looked upon it, and felt it with our hands; and it is of this we tell. Our theme is the word of life. *This life was made visible*; we have seen it and bear our testimony; we have declared to you the eternal life which dealt with the Father and was made visible to us. *What we have seen and heard we declare to you, so that you and we together may share a common life*, that life which we share with the Father and his Son Jesus Christ. *And we write this in order that the joy of us all may be complete.*' (1 John 1: vv. 1–4 NEB)

*   *   *

4

The Spirit in the religious life

John Lewis
Bishop of North Queensland, Australia

4

IT WAS IN THE OLD THEATRE ROYAL IN TOWNSVILLE AT THE END of 1972 that I had my first experience of the charismatic renewal. The theatre has now been pulled down and in its place stands a twenty-two storied building with a modern hotel on the ground floor and luxury apartments on the top. Before its demolition the Theatre Royal was often used for Church functions especially when people gathered to hear visiting speakers.

The occasion of this experience was an unusual one. We were having a healing mission in Townsville and the Anglican Church were co-sponsors with the Assemblies of God, a Pentecostal denomination. Two speakers had been invited to come: one was Canon Jim Glennon from the healing ministry in St. Andrew's Cathedral, Sydney, and the other was Pastor Norman Armstrong from the Abundant Life Centre in New South Wales. During the mission, mid-day services were held in St. James' Cathedral, and the evening sessions took place in the Theatre Royal. The Anglicans hosted the Cathedral services and the Assemblies took the platform in the evening. Such an alliance was new to North Queensland and to ensure its success, Canon Glennon agreed not to speak publicly on the Neo-Pentecostal Movement as it was then called.

The Spirit comes

Like all missions, this one was unpredictable and we all learned a very obvious lesson about preaching, namely, that whatever a preacher may or may not agree to do, in the end he is required to speak the Word of God. This is exactly what Canon Glennon did, and as a result we all received a blessing from the Spirit. Though he was not listed to preach on his last evening in Townsville, a request was made to him to give the final address, and this he did. Towards the end of his address, Canon Glennon suddenly burst into 'speaking in tongues', and with great dignity, an elderly man in the theatre rose and interpreted this beautiful and fulfilling prayer. What followed was amazing. Within an hour one of our Archdeacons and four Anglican nuns were speaking in tongues, and within a short time a number of other people were blessed in this way. The Charismatic Movement had arrived.

My own feelings should have been stirred, but I am afraid they were just the opposite. I felt calm and surprisingly warm inside. I was surprised at it all, but the moment Jim Glennon spoke in a tongue I knew that God was in it and that having tried to shield my people from this, I must now accept it gratefully. For the first time in my life I was acutely aware of the futility of our own plans and safeguards in the face of the power of God, who rules over all. What surprised me more than anything else was the way it all happened. Adults and even children were speaking in tongues and others were hoping for this experience to come to them; but there was nothing offensive about it at all. When this had gone on for about an hour I gave them a blessing and sent the Anglicans home to bed.

The odd thing was that I did not speak in a tongue myself. Later this gift came along with others as well, but on that evening in 1972 my feelings were different. The minute Canon Glennon spoke in his tongue I knew that things would begin happening. Then, after a moment of apprehension, I was made aware of the presence of the Spirit of Jesus. I felt at peace and committed all of us into the hands of the Spirit. Then a strange thing happened. My whole life seemed to come alive in a heavenly, warm light, rather like the light of a fire in a cosy room, and I felt myself looking through the past and quietly reviewing my spiritual life. Everything seemed safe in the fire light, and the discipline and burden of prayer that I used to find so difficult and onerous suddenly eased. I have always had a great devotion to Ignatius Loyola and his method of meditation but up to this moment it had seemed to me to be a strict, disciplined way to follow. Now the past disciplines of prayer seemed to pave the way forward and I felt not only secure in the lessons I had learnt, but directed forward into new areas of prayer which were not at variance with what had gone before. My past spiritual life had been revived and renewed.

Then came the next surprise. My prayers began to be answered in wonderful, though sometimes amusing, ways. I remember once standing shaving in the early morning and talking to the Lord about the Cathedral, which badly needed a new curate. Later in the morning a parish priest rang up to say that he no longer required his curate, and so the answer came. On another occasion I was going to Charters Towers, a city 90 miles to the west, for a confirmation, and at the time I dreaded the journey as I had an unpleasant tropical fever. My personal secretary and a priest staying at Bishop's Lodge both laid hands on me for healing, and off I went. The symptoms of the fever lingered for a few hours, but I made the journey and carried out the confirmation in reasonable comfort.

Most of the people involved in the Charismatic Movement speak in tongues, and they see this gift as an assurance of the renewal in their lives through the Spirit of Jesus. Certainly the gift of tongues is significant, but in my case it has been the gift of wisdom that has brought so many blessings to others and to me personally. Being a bishop brought up in the catholic tradition of the Anglican Church, I endeavoured to be impartial regarding the charismatic scene, and this may have inhibited the gift of tongues in my case. I received it alright, but only used it when praising God alone, and this I normally did in the car on long journeys about the diocese of North Queensland. With wisdom it was a different matter. It still is.

I became aware of the gift of wisdom when the Rev. Rodman Williams visited Townsville a few years ago. Up till that time no specific thoughts about the gift of wisdom had entered my head, but when Rodman Williams began explaining the meaning of the gift I was greatly moved. I knew the Hebrew concept of wisdom differed from the Greek, but I failed to see where the difference lay. I suddenly saw the wise man as one who knew the mind of God, and was able to explain this to people. The Greek concept was speculative, while the Hebrew one was instructive. To the Hebrew, the wise man knew the mind of God especially in relation to God's law or teaching, and the wise exercised their gift of wisdom in the way they explained this teaching. The Book of Proverbs is a good example of this. It is the same in our families. The wise child knows the mind of his or her parents and acts accordingly. Jesus was one who was so close to the mind of God that St. John described him as the 'mind made flesh'. Here the word is *logos* in Greek and embraces a range of meanings including 'word', 'reason', 'teaching', etc.

If the wise child knows the mind of the parent, it follows

that he knows what to do, and what is expected of him. It is the same with anyone who has the gift of wisdom. Such a person knows what God has in mind for him and others, and learns to do what is expected of him. The gift of wisdom is the clue to the will of God, and in exercising this gift, we learn to do the things God has in mind for us, and in some cases, for others.

We move forward

When people have experiences in the spiritual life they are often regarded with suspicion, and I certainly experienced this. Church life usually proceeds cautiously and when a few people get excited about something there is bound to be trouble. In North Queensland the trouble was short-lived, partly because of the orderly way in which people received the awakening, and partly because the spirit of renewal directed us all towards the ministry of the diocese. In my case, I found a new confidence in prayer, and with it the ability to ponder and work out the decisions I had to make and to bring them to fruition. Several prayer groups came into existence in Townsville and other parts, and we established a healing ministry in the Cathedral. Other priests found their ministries renewed and there was a spirit of confidence and thanksgiving in the air.

Wisdom

In my ministry as a bishop the gift of wisdom made it possible for me to begin directing the affairs of the diocese in a more acceptable fashion, as I now felt that I had a deeper knowledge of the will of God, and could carry it through with care and conviction. The office of Spiritual Director is well known in some parts of the Church, as it is a responsibility that falls to priests, but it is never easy to carry out. Religious folk often resent direction to the point of rudeness, and directors find themselves merely resorting to tentative suggestions or giving up in despair. A lot of this stems from the fact that Christianity has been on the defensive for so long that many have forgotten how to lead, and numbers of Christians refuse to be led. However, when renewal emerges, there is a willingness to move forward and to move out, and people then seek direction to point the way. We know the Spirit of Jesus leads us into the truth, and I believe I am being enabled now to lead my diocese into the way of truth. Moreover, I am able to do it without forcing people or resorting to shouting and temperamental outbursts. Naturally it is not all plain sailing, but the general situation is a great improvement on what had gone on before. It was a time of great expectation, for I found people expecting great things of me, and I of them in return. Expectation is a wonderful word, and is one of the mainstays of hope. Hope ceases to be wishful thinking when people resolutely form expectations in the Christian Life and set about achieving them.

Order

With this new sense of direction came a spirit of orderliness and this slowly pervaded everything. The diocese of North Queensland is on the frontier of the Anglican Church in Australia and, as it is about 700 miles deep and 600 miles long, it is difficult to keep together and to direct effectively. Though the towns are substantial in size and in services, they are far apart and, with the advent of the tropical wet season each year, the whole diocese can be bogged down with heavy rain and flooding or blown to pieces with cyclones. The weather, the distance, the lack of resources and the scarcity of trained personnel make it difficult to put things in order let alone maintain an orderly operation, and yet this is what has happened.

The first thing achieved was an administrative reform which made it possible to process diocesan business and make wise decisions for the future. The next achievement was a pastoral care programme which has introduced a new spirit of stewardship and visitation into the diocese. Currently we are working on a programme which will result in two groups being set up to plan the ministries and centres of ministry for the future and to prepare clear guidelines for the recruiting and training of the ministries of tomorrow.

Orderliness is a mark of the Spirit of Jesus, and is very evident in the New Testament especially in the accounts of Jesus feeding and teaching the multitudes, where, with a few men and some essential resources, he was able to minister to so many. The two great exponents of this in the Old Testament were Moses and Aaron, who not only led the people home from Egypt but ministered to their needs on the way. To bring orderliness to people, one has either to resort to force and persuasion or to stand in the power of the Spirit as Jesus did and as Moses and many others did before him.

As we became more aware of the presence of the Spirit in our lives, we noticed a new order of things and found the way forward much more fulfilling. Some of us felt moved to go to a seminar on Christian Management conducted by a devoted group of churchmen who specialise in this area, and in so doing we were able to identify the spiritual basis of the order in life and to see the way in which the servants of God operate.

I must stress again that none of these things happened easily, and along the path there were moments of apprehension and tension. Not everyone could see where we were going nor did they appreciate the means we were using to get there.

Visions

Another thing happened that was a little more difficult to cope with. In the last instance people do not mind direction nor do they mind the responsibility and accountability that come with orderliness, but visions are another matter. In the early stages of renewal in North Queensland, a number of people saw visions, especially of Jesus, and they found them most inspiring. Visions of the Lord may fill a person with deep respect and awe as Moses discovered in the desert, and they are beautiful things to share with friends who are in sympathy with such matters. To outsiders they are often a cause of deep concern and grave suspicion. Telling someone you have had a vision is tantamount, in many cases, to saying that you are suffering from a mental aberration, and this lack of sympathy and appreciation often puts the visionary in great spiritual jeopardy. When people do visualise deep spiritual issues they do need to share their treasures and if they are rejected they not only doubt their sanity but the very presence of the Spirit of Jesus who is the author of many visions. Of course the gift of discernment is needed to ensure that the vision is of the Lord, and the spirit of wisdom too to interpret it, for visions are capable of infinite interpretation and are often associated with the visionary's vocation and calling. The vision of Isaiah (Isaiah 6) is a case in point. Jews and Christians have pondered this vision for nearly 3,000 years, and countless disciples have found their calling in this vision just as Isaiah did.

My own experience of vision has been slight, and for

many years I relied on the visions of others, especially those recounted in the Bible. Visions first became important to me when I became a member of a religious order and discovered that the founder of the Order had a vision years ago of seeing the members of the Order as lighted candles brought into a church in such numbers that the whole church was full of light and warmth. Though the vision waned at the time of his receiving it, nevertheless it was and still is a source of great comfort to me. Then I had another experience that was quite different. On this occasion I was sent by my Society to take charge of an agricultural school in tropical Queensland for a few years, and on arrival I soon discovered that the school owned a herd of dairy cows. Production from the herd was low, so I employed a farm manager and set about buying better cows to improve the herd. I sought the farm manager's advice in this and he took me to see a cow of his that was almost the perfect animal. He remarked 'If you get that cow in the back of your eye you'll know what to look for when you go to buy new cattle.' After years spent with well-bred cattle he had a vision of the perfect cow, and this was how he passed it on to me. I did get a picture of the perfect cow in the back of my eye and it has been helpful to me ever since. So it is with Jesus. When we gaze on him in his word, in his sacraments and in the person of his followers, we come to a vision of Christ which draws us along the way of truth. The vision of Jesus helps us to see him in people and when shared, helps them to find him too.

While many around me have had visions of the Lord, and in some cases of the Virgin Mary, my own visions have centred on my work and ministry. At first I had a vision of our diocese as the Body of Christ along the lines of St. Paul's teaching in 1 Cor. 12; more recently I have begun to see the diocese as a family, and a few months ago at a diocesan rally at which many of our people were present, this vision of the diocesan family suddenly became a reality in a most moving fashion. I was standing at the altar watching the clergy administer Holy Communion to the great crowd when my vision suddenly came alive and I felt that the family had emerged.

There have been times when I have had to help others with their visions, and in one case this demanded a good deal of courage. It happened during a controversial debate in our Synod. A speaker was opposing a policy I favoured, and concluded his speech with a description of a vision he had had the previous night, which he felt confirmed his point of view. Many members of the Synod were embarrassed at the description of the vision and I was particularly annoyed because he opposed my own view in this way. The next day when pondering the vision in a calmer frame of mind, it suddenly came to me that it was a vision of God which did have a message of hope for the diocese. The vision identified cancerous growths in the diocese depicted as the Body of Christ, and encouraged me to recognise the reality of this sickness and to take steps to bring healing to the body. I telephoned the priest who had the vision, and after sharing together we were both reconciled and edified.

Things to forget

There have been some other insights which have come with this renewal, and three in particular are worthy of mention. Bishops normally live in large, old houses and the Lodge in Townsville is no exception. It is a lovely home, classified by the National Trust, with its own atmosphere and mystique. However, there is and always will be a dispatch problem. People often ring the Lodge with their problems, and it is not uncommon for me to bring quite a few problems home as well. The question is just what to do with all these problems and trouble. Some of them are capable of resolution because they arise from the work of the ministry, but others are made up of complaints and critical personal remarks that seem to come the way of all those committed to the ministry. There are times when the burden of these things becomes intolerable, but after renewal in the Spirit we were given a lead. My personal secretary was presented with a book by a dying friend, and the author was Norman Vincent Peale. One day when life was very tense, she read me a passage in which the author advises people to put all their cares in the waste-paper basket at the end of the day, just like a man cleaning all his pockets and throwing into the basket all the unnecessary bits and pieces. We tried it and it worked. Not everything can or should be discarded, but it is surprising how much can. The sense of release was wonderful and the Lodge is a different place now.

Throwing away the unnecessary cares and troubles of life does require a spirit of discernment and this we began to exercise in good measure. It is one thing to know what to put down, but it is another to know what to raise up. We found at Bishop's Lodge that there is a great temptation in life to forget the good things and to remember and brood over the bad. For example, someone is unkind and discourteous to you, and instead of letting this all fall into the wastepaper basket you often find yourself talking to others about it, pondering and churning it over, and in the end you finish up in a state of depression. This is what happens when you recall the bad things. If you let such things fall away and remember only the good things of life you are indeed living in the Spirit of Jesus. Life in the Spirit is a life of constant resurrection and to enjoy it we need to learn to recall good words, memories and ideas and reject the bad.

Norman Vincent Peale suggests that this experience can be quite enjoyable too, as we quietly throw away the unwanted things of life.

Gifts in the life of religious communities

It is now thirty years since I left the Navy and became involved in the life and work of a religious community. My bishop in Adelaide first introduced me to the Society of the Sacred Mission, which was starting a training college for the ministry in Adelaide, and having been accepted by them for training, I entered their college in St. Michael's House on the summit of Mount Lofty in South Australia. After a few months as a student, I applied to join the Society and having completed the novitiate I became a full member in 1951. To take life vows in a men's community was uncommon at the time in Australia, and my friends were noisily unsympathetic, though my family stood by me. The grounds of regret centred around the fact that I would never marry, and this certainly was a hard thing to accept. However, I found it even harder to accept the disciplined life of the Society and willingly to obey my superiors. Later when I became a superior I found it just as hard to get people to obey me. Obedience always seemed to be a battle of wills, with mine often at variance with the will of another, but this is only a symptom of a much deeper problem.

The way to approach this problem is to remember that our concern at all times should not be with our own will but with the will of God. Superiors and leaders have a double responsibility here. They have to find God's will for themselves and also God's will for those under their direction. Like Elisha in the Old Testament all superiors should ask for a double portion of the Spirit of God as they have at all times the double responsibility for themselves and for others. Just recognising that God's will is our goal is not sufficient. We have to know what it is. In my early days in the Society I was often told by the brothers that our founder, Fr. Kelly, had a stock reply to the question 'How do we know God's will?' He used to say, 'That's the giddy joke, we don't.' I never found this rejoinder very helpful and searched the scriptures, listened to the advice and direction of others and observed the events and incidents of life in the search for God's will. The exercise was not in vain, but it seemed to lack depth and I never carried out the Lord's will with the conviction I should have had. Then I received the blessing of the Spirit, and with this came the gift of wisdom.

Gifts are things we often receive but tend to put aside for future use. Wisdom is no exception in this. It is one of the gifts specifically named in confirmation and yet it was only after the renewal experience that I realised that I had the gift. If wisdom is what I believe it is, namely the gift of knowing the mind of God, then it is the sure way of finding his will. When we know his mind and what he expects of us, then we are able to settle down and carry out his will. It sounds very simple and in fact it is. This is probably the 'giddy joke' that Fr. Kelly often mentioned, and most of the time the joke is on us, for we give the impression that we have to think out what God's will is, when all the time we have the gift of wisdom to read his mind. This does not mean that we know everything in the mind of God, but we know sufficient for our own lives and for those for whom we are responsible.

The implications in the life of religious communities are enormous. An awareness of the gift of wisdom spells hope for every superior and leader and it brings fulfilment to those under direction. It applies equally in any family or group that is under direction in the service of God, and the exercise of the gift of wisdom not only gives us access to the will of God but it saves us all from 'doing our own thing'. In recent years this has been a significant feature in the religious life, where people have tried everything from the life of a hermit to a life of witness folding clothes in a local laundry. All of these things can be encompassed and embraced by the religious vocation in our communities and societies, but in the end an account of the work has to be given. The test of this account is whether or not the work and its fulfilment is the will of the Lord, and in doing the work and accounting for it, the gift of wisdom is needed. As a superior in a religious community for many years, I only had an inkling of this gift, and now that I am deeply aware of it, I do pray earnestly that all members of societies and communities receive this blessing. May we seek the stirring of the Spirit that the gift of wisdom may be ours not just to receive and store up but to use boldly all the days of our lives.

Freedom and order

One of the dreams of the religious person in a society is of a life which is disciplined, orderly and well structured. There are times in community life when this is so and there are times when the very opposite happens. There are a multitude of reasons for disorder in life. The management of the community may be weak and ineffective, or the house may be large and unmanageable, or again, the demands of the work may be beyond the capacity of the society members, or perhaps the aims of the society are outmoded and no longer helpful. Whatever the cause, the fact remains that the religious life in a community is not always an orderly life and the consequences of disorder can be painful in the extreme. Just to meet the challenge of disorder with the remark that the Holy Spirit will put things right is hardly sufficient, but at least it is a move in the right direction. The Spirit performs two functions that help to bring order – namely to strengthen and to lead. When people are called to worship or serve together in a way of life as intimate and close as the religious life, the need for strength is essential if the life is to function harmoniously. I am not referring here only to physical strength, but also the inner strength to follow and walk in the way of Jesus. Every time someone falls down or collapses on the way, their burden has to be shared out, and constant and chronic collapses can and do bring disorder and confusion in the life of any group. Now the Holy Spirit is referred to by St. John as the Comforter or Strengthener, and the presence and prompting of the Spirit is a great source of strength in the religious life. Jesus' reference to the Spirit as a spring of water bubbling up within us is helpful here, for the Spirit does rise up within us and give us the strength, physically and spiritually, to achieve the tasks required of us.

The Spirit also leads us into the truth. When the Spirit of Jesus leads us, or in some cases drives, there is no confusion. I often think of the cleansing of the temple in this connection. Our Leader took the initiative and drove out the merchants and their stock and animals. If the task had been committed to the disciples no doubt there would have been confusion and chaos with birds and animals all over the place. As it was, the whole operation happened in an orderly fashion with no mention of confusion. Driving is an aggressive form of leadership, used mainly in emergencies, and this incident highlights the mark of Jesus' leadership, which is to direct people along the appropriate way for them, and for the merchants, that way lay outside. This is the way the Spirit of Jesus leads us. He guides and directs people into the way of Jesus who is the Truth. It is a living way, marked by orderliness and admits of no confusion.

To follow this way and enjoy this orderly life, one must be a disciple of Jesus empowered by the Spirit. Discipleship is rare in the modern Church because people are not anxious to be led, nor are they willing to accept the discipline of attending to the Lord, receiving and pondering his word and following in his way of service. Where discipleship is weak, discipline is poor and life is unsettled. But when disciples are dedicated, the discipline is apparent and life flows on harmoniously.

Order comes from the strength and leadership of the Spirit of Jesus, and when we recognise this source and this authority we are well on the way. To imagine that being a so-called tough disciplinarian, or to shout out orders is going to bring discipline and order in life is to make a serious mistake, and when leaders resort to such methods the results are short-lived and usually unpleasant. But to wait on the Spirit of Jesus with expectancy will release his strength and leadership in our lives and in our service. My advice to religious societies and communities is that they should ensure that their rules and constitutions are in keeping with their life and work today, and that they should pray earnestly to the Holy Spirit for strength and leadership so that discipline and true orderliness may be a constant mark of the religious life in the church.

More about visions

When it comes to visions, most religious communities are not lacking. My own Society has always had Fr. Kelly's vision of the darkened church and the bringing in of the lights, and other communities have various visions to inspire their members. I can remember once at a religious life conference at Oxford, talking to a well-known Mother Superior and a noted theologian, when a Sister passed by wearing a most elaborate headdress. At the time the winds of change were blowing through the Church, and complicated headdresses were decidedly out. The Mother Superior, in answer to our comments on this unsuitable headgear, pointed out that the founder of the community in question had had a vision of the Virgin Mary wearing such a headdress and the present day Sisters were stuck with it. I have no doubt people in religious communities could tell many such stories, and these would go to show that visions are not only known but they often have a profound effect on the life-style and service of a community.

The question then arises about the occurrence of such visions in the future. It is one thing for the founder to have a vision, but it is quite another for successive generations of monks, nuns and religious to have visions also. And yet they do, and granted the need for discernment, the visions will not conflict when they are inspired by the Spirit of Jesus. For example, in our Australian house, one brother had a vision of the garden, which he followed so that it became like Eden. Another had a vision of food and its preparation which nearly earned him a Cordon Bleu certificate, while yet another had a vision of the library. Other visions related to the Society, its theological tradition and its new concepts of preparing men for lay ministry. These visions are like pictures in the mind of God, and without them it is difficult to see how a person can move forward. We are all familiar with Joel's comments on the outpouring of the Spirit, when the mature persons look back over their dreams and the younger ones enjoy their visions. This is the way it must be in the life of a religious community and such groups should pray to the Lord to receive from the Spirit of

Jesus visions that will inspire their members to worship, praise and serve the Lord in all areas of the Christian life.

Looking back over my experience in the Charismatic Movement, I am aware of many blessings that have come my way, and have often been made aware of God's blessings for others. I have never felt moved to commit others to my way of thinking in this, but have hoped and prayed that they would receive the confidence to reach out and use the gifts the Spirit is offering them. In my life the gifts of wisdom and order have been paramount, and I seem consistently to encounter visions in the lives of others. I do pray that in the Church of today Christians will enjoy these gifts and in particular that Religious Orders will receive them and utilise them to the full in the service of Jesus our Saviour.

*   *   *

5

The Spirit and worship

Richard Hare
Bishop of Pontefract, England

5

He has put a new song in my mouth . . . Many shall see it and fear.
                                                              Psalm 40

IT WAS IN 1971, SHORTLY AFTER I HAD BECOME A BISHOP, THAT various friends urged me to take note of the fact that something new of great significance was happening in the Church. Father Bernard Chamberlain, of the Community of the Resurrection, persevered with me. I owe him a debt of gratitude. There have been many other renewal movements in the Church, but my friends stressed that the new and significant feature about this one was that it was happening within the institutional structures themselves, and had not been forced into exile. So I took to going to renewal meetings whenever they would have me, very conscious of being an outsider, simply to urge them not to go underground, or into orbit, or be more peculiar than they could help. My standard gambit used to be: 'Greetings from the dry bones': and I used to tell them that it is all very well for the renewal to say 'The structures need renewal', but I came to say 'The renewal needs the structures'. I used to point out that it is no good simply quoting from the story of Ezekiel's vision: 'Come from the four winds, O breath, and breathe upon these slain', for if there are no bones for the breath to come into the whole thing is a load of hot air. I used to go as a kind of representative dry bone, until, without my realising it was going to happen, I found myself personally involved too. I had for a long time thought that I was too middle-class, too up-tight and inhibited, and just not that sort of person: no one was more surprised than me.

When it happened, the familiar results followed; the scriptures came alive in a remarkable way, I found a new desire for prayer, a fresh delight in the company of my fellow Christians, and a release of joy and praise within me that I would not have believed possible. Since then I have become aware of several strands within the renewal, in addition to the emphasis on spiritual gifts (particularly healing, tongues, and prophecy), which first strikes those who are in touch with what is going on, but are still conscious of being outsiders. There is, for instance, the seemingly insatiable appetite for solid teaching evidenced by the large sale of books and tapes, not all of the basic testimony kind. I noticed that during a recent Fountain Trust conference the tapes of all the lectures were being sold in large numbers as fast as they were put out on the tables: upwards of six thousand tapes were sold during the week. There is too, on the part of the people involved, the desire for personal growth, and the search for a spiritual wholeness and maturity which has hitherto eluded them. This can be seen in a willingness to be totally frank in seeking for advice and prayer-counsel, and also in the willingness to find out from those with experience of it what is involved in various forms of contemplative prayer. There are also the manifestations of renewal within the ordered worship of our churches, and it is this release of liturgical spontaneity and whoopee which is the subject of this chapter.

One thing to note at the outset is that charismatic worship can go on for a very long time. The Eucharist can, for instance, last for all of three hours, without the participants having any sense that it has been inordinately long: though possibly some who have attended from a sense of duty or curiosity may have felt otherwise! One can frequently be refreshed, where in the past one was merely thrown by the unexpected. I well remember being in the vestry of a Pentecostal Church in Texas, along with the pastor and fifteen or so of the elders, and hearing the pastor say: 'Shall we have a word of prayer?' The phrase brought back memories of Free Church vestries during the Week of Prayer for Christian Unity, when someone would attempt an off-the-cuff collect of the 'O Lord thou knowest that we are here . . .' variety. I bowed my head reverently, prepared for something similar: but not a bit of it. Instead we all put our heads down and linked shoulders like a football scrum, and all prayed aloud at the same time: a few in tongues, some in articulate English, and some confining themselves to short but frequent ejaculations. We all knew instinctively when the prayer was over, straightened up and went in to start the service. I learned afterwards that this is called 'praying with one accord'. I felt it was a long way from 'O Lord open thou our lips', but this was in fact precisely what the Lord had done. Imagine the consternation there would be in some churches if the Lord were to take us literally!

The exciting thing is that we are witnessing the renewal of the Church in the power of the Holy Spirit, and are not concerned just with furtherance of a 'movement'. We are not, by our efforts, renewing the Church. Nevertheless it is certainly true that clumsy and insensitive behaviour on our part can set back the cause of renewal. I have been taught that when things go flat, in a prayer group, a congregation, or in our own devotional life, the first thing to look for is an absence of praise, and then an unwillingness in commitment. But when things go bizarre we should look at once for a failure in ministry. One of the public manifestations of renewal will be within the ordered worship of the Church, and it calls for really sensitive ministry and leadership to ensure that this is neither stifled nor allowed to divide the congregation into sheep and goats, leaving one group with a deep sense of rejection.

Perhaps at this point I could say what great support I have found from belonging to a prayer group composed of people actively involved in the ministry. I have been able to go to a number of such groups from time to time as a visitor, some entirely Anglican, some mixed, and I have seen what a help it has been to those who are normally in leadership roles to be ministered unto by each other in such groups. Those I have attended have for the most part been eucharistic groups, meeting for prayer and sacrament during the course of a morning. They have been conducted with a good deal of informality, within the basic structure of the eucharistic form. The ministry of the word has taken the form of a discussion, and likewise the intercession has lasted for as long as those present still had people and concerns which they wanted the group to bring before the Lord. There has been the opportunity to share in confidence matters of deep perplexity or sorrow or penitence; also the chance to share in each other's joy when there have been occasions of special blessing. Usually the sacrament has been passed from one to another round the circle, and there has been singing and the chance to express the deep sense of fellowship which regular participation in such a group engenders. If you belong to a Church which has bishops, and if you yourself belong to such a group as I have described, let me urge you to involve your bishop in it if you possibly can. It is very easy to be isolated by reverence, and if renewal is going to make progress in episcopal Churches it is vital that the bishops themselves be drawn in.

I have personally found it of enormous value to be allowed to belong to one group of this kind, composed of people of widely different ages and levels of seniority, and to belong to it as one regular member among others.

Within this group I have received more ministry than I have given, and have felt myself to be 'earthed' in the ordinary life of the Church in such a way as is not always possible for a bishop. It is true that some clergy have always sheltered behind the role, taken refuge behind a cardboard figure of a clergyman and made the right noises from there; but I believe it is more common to find the institution pushing its ministers into that position, because people have found it safer and less disconcerting to relate to a cardboard figure than to a real person. So it has been with bishops. I do not believe that bishops have often isolated themselves. But I do believe that they have often been isolated by the Church to which they have tried to minister. So if your Church is experiencing renewal, and if you have a bishop, let me urge you to think of ways of enabling him to share in such an experience. Do not treat him as someone who simply has to be brought in when there is trouble, or for great occasions. Write and ask for his prayers when there is something about to happen which means a lot to you, or when there is a decision to be taken and the congregation is uncertain what to do. If you are having a weekend of renewal, or a parish retreat, ask the bishop if you can bring the leader over to meet him so that he can pray with him and bless him and his ministry before it starts. Your letter will make a welcome contrast among the plethora of routine business that lands on his desk each morning!

Our concern is with the renewal of the Church, not with the creation of a sect within the Church. We must reckon with the fact that the liberation of the Church's worship, which will be one feature of its renewal, is likely to cause at least apprehension in some deeply entrenched quarters. Some years ago a cartoon showed a sour-faced clergyman looking over the pulpit at his suitably respectful con-

gregation, and saying: 'I don't know who it was interrupted
our worship last Sunday with the words 'Praise the Lord',
but in future will he kindly remember that this is the House
of God and not do that again.' Anglicans seeing the cartoon
took it for granted that it portrayed an Anglican Church,
but those who have been around a good deal will know that
it could just as well have been any other: even one where
the pastor says 'Alleluia', and the congregation responds
'Praise the Lord', with about as much spontaneity as when
an Anglican congregation makes the appropriate response
to 'O Lord open thou our lips'.

There are many people who long, deep down, to be
spontaneous in their worship as elsewhere: but somehow
they cannot quite bring themselves to let go. It should not
be hard to see why they feel resentful when they find in
someone else the spontaneity which they have not been
able to achieve. This has been at the root of the tension in
many parishes where renewal has threatened to split the
congregation.

Let us consider a typical Anglican parish, where renewal
has begun. A 'Thursday evening fellowship' has been
formed, and there have been no problems. So far as the rest
of the parish is concerned a few eccentrics have met
together, who like that kind of thing, and the wind has
blown where it listed. If it is not your scene you stay away.

After a while the group grows larger, and its effects begin
to be felt on Sunday morning worship. In many parishes we
then begin to see the signs of strain. There is apprehension.
There are the regulars, and the regular abstainers when it
comes to a time of free prayer. There are the refugees
scattered abroad among the other congregations of the
town. A threatened look appears when we arrive at the
Peace. Or we see the effect of a guitar-case in the vestry on
a choir which sings 'Our mouth shall show forth thy praise'

in such a way as to leave no doubt whose mouth they have in mind.

All of us hope and pray that renewal in the Spirit will make us progressively more sensitive to other people's feelings and tender spots. It takes all sorts to make a Church, and one sign of spiritual maturity, in an individual or in a congregation, is to be seen in the unthreatened acceptance of styles of spirituality which contrast with our own. Another is the desire to avoid shedding our inhibitions in such a way as to put off people who are still rather gingerly taking the temperature of the water before deciding whether to plunge in or not.

There is no doubt that to be with a lot of switched-on Christians, arms in the air and dancing round the Holy Table, when you are not switched-on yourself not only leaves you switched-off but also makes you feel positively excluded. And yet if nobody makes a move we shall never escape from the cut-and-dried pattern of totally predictable worship where many of the newly-released feel completely stifled. So what do we do?

First let us recognise that greater freedom in worship calls for the exercise of really positive ministry, and particularly for discernment with regard to gifts and their origin. Zion is a refuge for the wild goats, as well as for the coneys: in a renewed Church we shall always find a number of highly dependent people, much in need of support and spiritual massage, and we shall also find a lot of volatile enthusiasts whose exuberance can all too easily rip the whole thing apart if there is no effective control. We should rejoice that such people, who do not always find easy acceptance elsewhere, are drawn to our worship: but effective ministry will ensure that the tone of the worship is not set simply by them.

It has been frequently said that, besides the inspired

hunch, there are objective criteria to be used in practising discernment with regard to prophecy and interpreted tongues: *kērygma*, *agapē*, and *oikodomē*. The same criteria could be used in assessing the validity of our worship. Does it proclaim the good news of what God has done in Christ? Is it consistent with revealed truth as tested by scripture? Is it pervaded throughout by the love of God, shed abroad in our hearts by the Holy Spirit whom he has given us? Does it build up, or does it divide, the fellowship of believers? If it fails in respect of any of these four, then the answer, as with prophecy or interpreted tongues, is that it is phoney.

The vicar of a church where it was all beginning to happen was recently given some advice by the quietly forceful vicar of a neighbouring parish, where it had all been happening for some time: 'Watch out for the charismatic gipsies.' There will always be some who have not yet been properly integrated into a congregation, who are shopping around for opportunities to make their contribution where it has been reported that the reins are loose. Such people can set back the cause of renewal by years.

We must be sensitive to the need for freedom and spontaneity to be given liturgical expression within the general terms in which our own worshipping tradition has been developed. Some years ago David du Plessis was addressing a vast gathering of Roman Catholic charismatics. This was in the days when the Catholic renewal was in its early stages, and he took for his theme: 'Be ye not conformed to Pentecostalism, but be ye transformed by the renewing power of the Holy Spirit within your own tradition.' This is surely advice we should all heed. We want to provide an opportunity for liberty of expression, but to do it without so breaking continuity with the tradition in which people have grown up as to alienate those who do not yet feel their need for it.

I remember in the earlier nineteen fifties hearing of a parish which had, with careful teaching and great sen-sitivity, gone over from a matins tradition to parish com-munion every Sunday. The vicar felt at the end of the operation that he could truthfully say: 'Of all that you gave me I have lost none.' May it be so now! It will not be enough for a handful of joyful enthusiasts who have even-tually got their way to say to those who left: 'We piped to you and you did not dance.'

We must constantly remind ourselves that the Church is being renewed by the Lord, in the power of the Holy Spirit, and that its renewal is not something for which we our-selves are ultimately responsible. We may, for instance, long for the congregation of which we ourselves are a part to know the freedom and delight of 'singing in the Spirit', which is something outside the experience of worshippers in most traditional congregations. If we are impatient about this, and attempt to contrive the occasion before the people are ready, we will only increase resistance to this kind of liturgical freedom, and make people even more convinced than they already were that charismatic expres-sion in worship is utterly bizarre. On the other hand when the congregation is ready, it is possible that nothing will happen until there is a gentle nudge from those who are leading the worship. It is vital for them to cultivate the Quaker ability to discern the sense of the meeting, so that they will know when the mood is just right: for to share in this particular experience has often been the first taste of liberation for many people. The leader can, when he is sure that a nudge is all that is needed, suggest that the con-gregation hangs on to the last note of a suitable hymn or chorus, an alleluia perhaps gives the easiest opportunity, and pray that the Lord will loosen their tongues, so that they can praise him with the freedom that comes from him.

Another way in which congregations have found initial freedom from the rigidity of their liturgical structure has been in the creative use of silence. Silence in the liturgy has all too often been like space in the building, someone immediately wonders what would look nice there. But it need not be like that. Silence has often provided the first taste of freedom, and been the occasion for the dove to spread his wings. On the other hand with insensitive leadership silence can easily become the occasion for unease and embarrassment.

There must be many people who have held back from the rich experience of shared prayer because of early memories which put them off. I can myself look back to Christian Union meetings in my early teens, when we sat round in a large circle and were expected to pray aloud in turn. I remember longing for the courage which was said to have enabled one robust individualist to say 'Pass', as I sat cringing and waited for the creeping barrage to hit me. Or else we may retain memories of seemingly endless extempore prayers, which, as Bernard Manning once said, went on so long that the people in the congregation were at the end like native villagers coming out of their huts after a tornado to see who was missing and who was still there. If only the person praying had known the pungent advice given to lengthy preachers: 'Even if you cannot finish, you can always stop!'

In a prayer group, or in a time of free prayer and intercession in the liturgy, two or three can be briefed to prime the pump, and to do so in such a way as to offer an easy formula for the diffident: 'Lord, remember Susan, who is having an operation on Tuesday', 'Lord remember John and Mary, who are emigrating to Australia', 'Lord, remember Margaret, who has lost her husband', etc. In quite a short time this can generate its own spontaneity, and people for whom the formula was the way in will find that they want to pray in words of their own choosing.

The extended Peace can also be a point of break-through for a congregation, hitherto resistant to any kind of freedom of expression. Two things are important. The people must realise that what is being shared does not consist only of their own friendliness and goodwill: they are sharing the peace of the Lord. Also it is vital that a number of people be briefed not to look for their own friends, but instead to be aware of those who do not seem to know anybody, or even may not want to know anybody. There must have been countless instances when the extended Peace has been an occasion of painful isolation for some of those who most needed the love of others.

The current renewal is taking place within existing ecclesiastical institutions. This is the new factor. There are certainly new Christians, in large numbers, but they are being brought into the worshipping life of congregations whose liturgical forms have developed their own rigidity over the years, and are not joining sects whose spiritual awareness only slightly ante-dates their own. We believe that the Holy Spirit is teaching us how to pray, both in our corporate liturgy and in our private inner life, and is leading us to a freedom in worship which is a new experience for many of us. It is important for those in leadership roles to be entirely relaxed themselves, seeking all the time to co-operate with the Lord rather than to manipulate the situation in line with the blue-print they have adopted. They must also learn certain basic techniques by which those tensions can be relaxed which inevitably develop when one section of the congregation has been renewed and the other has not. The two great relaxers of tension are

humour, and confident gentleness. Gentleness which is not
confident relaxes nobody but simply makes everyone ill at
ease: confidence which is not gentle puts everyone's back
up. But confident gentleness, combined with sensitive
humour, can be used to take the fizz out of a potentially
disruptive situation. Anyone who has ever seen Canon
Harry Sutton at work will know the kind of skill I have in
mind. Canon Sutton himself could charm the birds off the
trees, and the vital thing for the rest of us to learn from him
is that effective humour in this connection never, never
hurts anyone.

To be specific, rather than attempt to theorise about the
role of the Spirit in worship, the crunch, in many Anglican
parishes anyway, has come when *Fresh Sounds, Sound of
Living Waters*, and *Psalm Praise* began to spill over from
Thursday night to Sunday morning. Then in many parishes
people could be seen bracing themselves for a trial of
strength, lobbying support for their cause, and preparing
themselves to sit down and be counted. This is where the
bond of love must really take the strain, and the young
must show genuine concern and gentleness for the
middle-aged and elderly.

My impression, borne out by everyone I have spoken to
about it, is that when they are confronted with the real fruit
of the Spirit in young people, older Christians, however
different their cultural outlook, are the first to thank God
for the freedom with which younger people praise the
Lord, and which they are being invited to share. I well
remember being at a service of considerable freedom, and
noticing that afterwards when tea and coffee were being
drunk, there were ladies in stockings, gloves, and hats
talking with animated interest to young men and girls in
sandals and jeans and what could only be described as
vests. Each saw the point of the other, and the worshipping

fellowship was enriched and strengthened by the mixture. But if older people are confronted with something strident which seems to be aimed at them, then their gift of discernment is probably not far out if, in what purports to be worship, they sense their own rejection. When this happens we should first look to see if there has been a failure in ministry and leadership.

The Lord is renewing his Church, we believe, with a recovery of its sense of urgency in mission, and a restoration of its unity. This is being manifested in several ways. One way is the loosening and refreshment of its worshipping life, which now so often transcends the traditional barriers of denominational allegiance, and is outward-looking in its proclamation that Jesus is Lord of all. It is important for this renewal movement to retain the affection and trust of those who feel threatened by the changes.

It is significant that in the Fourth Gospel it was the raising of Lazarus ('Loose him and let him go') that was the last straw so far as the forces of law and order were concerned. Of course freedom and spontaneity are dangerous, like leaving the boat to walk on the water, but it is through liberated worship that the Lord is making his purpose known, and his people are being renewed. Let us open the cage, but not damage the contents!

* * *

6

The spiritual gifts

Chiu Ban It
Bishop of Singapore

6

'WALK, WALK, IN THE NAME OF JESUS – WALK!', THE EVANGEL~
IST said confidently to the man standing in front of him, and
I saw a man stagger towards me in the chancel without
crutches. He had not walked for a number of years, as a
result of injuries inflicted on him when he was in a Japanese
prisoner of war camp. I wanted to stretch out my hands to
catch him, but he steadied himself and walked towards me
awkwardly; *but he was walking.* People began to praise
God all around him. Some applauded as I walked alongside
him from the chancel down the side aisle of the Cathedral
before I left him to make his own unaided way accompanied by his wife and the friends who had brought him to
the service, back up the main aisle to his seat in the front
pews. This was only one of the many dramatic events which
took place during a five week period in June and July 1973
when services of 'Prayers for Healing' were held in some of
our Anglican Churches in Singapore, but specially at St.
Andrew's Cathedral itself.

The services attracted big crowds even though there was
no publicity. The Cathedral was crammed with 'all sorts
and conditions of people' including those who came in
wheel-chairs and with crutches. It seemed that the majority
were not Christians. The Cathedral had never in our
experience seen such happenings. Some of our members
were pleased that they were ministered to at last. Others
were offended. The main controversy, however, centred

round the 'healings'. It is true that in proportion to those who came for healing, the number who claimed to be healed was not very high, but they were sufficient to bring the crowds. Among the perplexing questions asked were 'can these claims of healing be substantiated, or are they illusions or even frauds?' 'Were they of God even if they were done in the Name of Jesus?' 'What about those who were not healed?'

Spiritual Gifts and the Anglican Church in Singapore

It was a bewildering and difficult time for me as bishop, because in 1972 there had been news that some groups of students in a few of the Church schools in Singapore had claimed that they had been 'baptised in the Holy Spirit' and some of their members had 'spoken in tongues'. These claims were beginning also to be made by some of the laity – and even some clergy of the main denominational Churches. I had decided not to do anything about this news and advised the few who asked me 'to ignore for the time being what appeared to be fanaticism' and quoted Gamaliel's advice that if it is of man it will fail but 'if it is of God, you will not be able to overthrow them'. (Acts 5: vv. 38 & 39).

I had no reason to question the view generally accepted by theologians that the 'spiritual gifts' referred to by Paul in 1 Cor. 12 had ceased to operate after the time of the Apostles. I had no experience of them, nor was I interested in finding out about them. I didn't really know what 'speaking in tongues' was.

By June 1973 however, I could no longer ignore what was happening. The services of 'Prayers for Healing' were attracting too much attention. Clergy as well as laity were coming to me for direction about the phenomena. When I was consecrated bishop in that very Cathedral I had been solemnly asked 'Will you then faithfully exercise yourself in the same Holy Scriptures, and call upon God by prayer, for the true understanding of the same, so as you may be able by them to teach and exhort with wholesome doctrine to withstand and convince gainsayers?' and answered 'I will do so, by the help of God.' I had very seriously to investigate the whole matter of 'spiritual gifts' and provide some answers.

Moreover, I had found myself unexpectedly experiencing privately six months earlier in January 1973 what I was told was a 'baptism in the Holy Spirit', 'speaking in tongues' in private, and now in full glare of the public was becoming a channel for the Holy Spirit's 'gifts of healing'.

Speaking in various kinds of tongues

It happened while I was attending an International Christian Conference in Bangkok in December 1972/January 1973. An Indian Anglican priest from Fiji gave me Dennis Bennett's *Nine o'clock in the Morning* to read. Certain aspects of the conference had got me down. The thrust of the conference seemed to me to be that Christians should let the 'world write the agenda' and Churches could only get things done by resorting to worldly power in its various worldly aspects. Salvation was through worldly means and only incidentally through the Gospel of Jesus Christ. There was naturally a good deal of heated debate among the speakers and delegates. It was, therefore, a relief to read Dennis Bennett's book about the love and power of God in action in the world today, in spite of my initial scepticism at what I was reading.

My rational mind was repelled by the descriptions of
'speaking in tongues', 'healings' and miraculous happenings.

'It's a fairy tale – they can't happen today!' was my first
reaction. At the same time, I was so fascinated and exhila-
rated by what I was reading that I could not put the book
down. When I finished the book it was time for an afternoon siesta. I prayed a short prayer:

'Lord please give me your Holy Spirit as you gave him to
Dennis Bennett and others mentioned in the book.'

I then dozed off.

When I woke up I was conscious of a great difference
within me. God was suddenly very close. My heart was
filled with love, joy and peace, instead of anger, despair
and gloom. I burst out with praise and thanked God
through Jesus Christ. When I ran out of English words I
resorted to Chinese. Soon I was struggling again to find the
words and correct theological thoughts to express myself.
The dam of the mind burst and I found myself uttering new
sounds and syllables which had no meaning to my mind but
which I knew in my spirit were fluently giving expression to
the praise and thanksgiving which was welling up within me
towards God. When I went under the shower the syllables
winged themselves into song!

Surprised and a little non-plussed by the experience, I
sought out my Indian friend and related to him what had
happened. Later he arrived in my room with a black
American Pentecostal minister and a Mexican Pentecostal
bishop. They asked me to share with them what had happened. We soon found ourselves on our knees, praying and
worshipping God simultaneously in a harmony of international and spiritual sounds! 'Jerusalem on the day of
Pentecost must have sounded like that,' I thought. When it

was over my friends assured me that I had been 'baptised in the Holy Spirit' and had been given the 'gift of speaking in tongues'. In fact, after the initial cross-examination we all began worshipping, praying and singing in tongues together! It was an awesome and reverent but joyful and beautiful experience.

The gift of the Holy Spirit

Up till then I had not seen much significance in the term 'baptism in the Holy Spirit'. True it is recorded in all four Gospels that John the Baptiser had pointed to Jesus and called him 'the Lamb of God', and 'this is he who baptises with the Holy Spirit', (John 1: v. 33). Jesus himself just before he ascended promised his disciples, 'for John baptised with water, but before many days you shall be baptised with the Holy Spirit.' Acts 1: v. 5.

I was certain that I had the Holy Spirit within me before this experience and was already saved, for it is the Holy Spirit who enabled me to confess to the world that 'Jesus is Lord' (1 Cor. 12: v. 3), and 'believe in my heart that God raised him from the dead.' (Rom. 10: v. 9). I was equally confident that I was already a son of God because I could confidently cry 'Abba, Father' through the Holy Spirit who was within me, (Rom. 8: vv. 14 & 15). These together with the outward evidences of my baptism and confirmation were sufficient to assure me that God the Holy Spirit was with me. Nevertheless, that afternoon I became intensely aware of the presence of God the Father and God the Son in the person of the Holy Spirit in a way I never had before. My friends called it the 'baptism in the Holy Spirit' but I feel that in the light of the above reasons, my experience should be described as a 'filling of the Holy Spirit' and that my colleagues and I that afternoon were 'filled with the

Holy Spirit' as in Acts 4: v. 31. However, I shall use the term 'to be baptised in the Holy Spirit' in this chapter as it is a biblical phrase and in common use.

That afternoon I learnt that I could remain constantly aware in my spirit of the presence of the Holy Spirit even though my mind might not be able to. I began to experience deeply the reality that the Spirit of Truth 'guides us into all truth' and at all times 'glorifies' Jesus the only begotten Son of God and our Saviour and Redeemer (John 16: vv. 13 & 14). For the first time I learnt that if I was ready to allow him to use me as a channel to manifest the 'spiritual gifts', for example the nine set out by Paul in 1 Cor. 12: vv. 8–10, whenever he wills, 'for the common good', he would graciously do so. They were supernatural gifts not merely heightened natural abilities.

I have often been asked how I could be so sure that what I had been filled with on that day was the Holy Spirit and not any other spirit. My certainty is based on Luke 11. It is recorded there that when Our Lord 'had ceased praying in a certain place one of his disciples said to him "Lord, teach us to pray." ' In reply he taught them what we have come to know as the 'Lord's Prayer'. He went on to promise them 'And I tell you, ask, and it will be given you; seek, and you will find; knock, and it will be opened to you.' v. 9. Then he asked 'What father among you, if his son asks for a fish will, instead of a fish, give a serpent; or if he asks for an egg will give a scorpion?' He concluded this teaching on prayer with the categorical statement 'If you being evil know how to give good gifts to your children, how much more will the heavenly Father give the Holy Spirit to those who ask him!' (Luke 11: v. 13).

In view of this can anyone who knows by faith that he is a child of God through Jesus Christ doubt for a moment that it is the Holy Spirit that he received when he has asked the

Father, in the name of Jesus Christ, to give him that same Spirit?

As a corollary, however, we have found by experience that it is always wise before praying for anyone to be baptised in the Holy Spirit or filled with the Holy Spirit to follow the advice of Peter to the crowds in Jerusalem on the day of Pentecost, as closely as possible, namely to ask that person to 'Repent and be baptised . . . in the name of Jesus for the forgiveness of your sins,' if the person has not already done so, and inviting him if he has already been baptised to make an act of personal re-commitment to Jesus Christ as his Lord and Saviour, so that the rest of the advice 'and you shall receive the gift of the Holy Spirit' may follow, 'for the promise is to you . . . and to all that are far off, every one whom the Lord our God calls to him.' (Acts 2: vv. 38 & 39). Otherwise there is the risk of the person receiving a wrong spirit.

When I returned to Singapore, I was determined to learn more about this new and invigorating experience. What could I find out about the 'baptism in the Holy Spirit'? What did 'speaking in tongues' mean? What about the other 'spiritual gifts' set out in 1 Cor. 12? Can they really be experienced today as Dennis Bennett asserts in his book? I was determined to keep my novel experience secret if possible, while I did some research on the subject, but it was not to be.

I concluded that the vivid awareness of the presence of God which remained with me and continues to do so had something profound to do with 'the baptism of the Holy Spirit'. I became very conscious of the Holy Spirit guiding me as I said my daily prayers and services and they ceased to be matters of duty but of real joy. Each Eucharist has become charged with the presence of our Lord in a new way. The confirmation service where the bishop first

prays that 'Almighty and everlasting God who has vouch-
safed to regenerate these thy servants by water and the
Holy Spirit' will 'strengthen them . . . with the Holy Spirit,
the comforter, and daily increase in them thy manifold gifts
of grace . . .' and then lays hands on each of them praying
that he will 'daily increase in thy Holy Spirit more and
more until he comes unto thy everlasting kingdom', has
become an inspiring occasion each time I am privileged to
take it.

I was thirsty to know more about the person and work of
the Holy Spirit but alas my commentaries and theological
books could give little or no help, especially on the
'spiritual gifts' namely 'the utterance of wisdom', the
'utterance of knowledge', 'faith', 'gifts of healing', 'working of miracles', 'various kinds of tongues' and 'interpretation of tongues' which St. Paul said are all 'inspired by
one and the same Spirit who apportions to each one individually as he wills.' (1 Cor. 12: vv. 8–11).

New avenues of instruction, however, opened up. Our
Lord's promise in John 16: v. 12 that 'when the Spirit of
Truth comes, he will guide you into all truth' began to be
fulfilled in remarkable ways. I was brought into touch with
a local Methodist pastor who during a severe sickness
experienced the saving presence of the Lord and found
himself suddenly speaking in tongues. His physicians
thought he had suddenly become delirious! Through him I
met the Rev. Hugh Baker an Assemblies of God missionary in Singapore. Others who could teach us about
spiritual gifts unexpectedly stopped by in Singapore. They
included Father E. Stube, an Episcopalian priest, who
knew the Rev. Dennis Bennett and was one of the early
group of American Anglicans who had entered into the
deeper experience of the Holy Spirit. Stube had for the past
8 years been teaching and ministering the spiritual gifts

with gratifying results in Indonesia. He gave us invaluable help and teaching on that subject.

Then came these dramatic services of 'prayers for healing' in our churches and at the Cathedral. People were being healed right before my very eyes. Suddenly I found that as I took part in the laying on of hands, I also became a 'messenger boy' for the Holy Spirit, delivering 'gifts of healing' to a person with a migraine, another who was deaf and to another who had asthma. I could not deny my experience of either 'tongues' or 'gifts of healing' but must admit that I still sought to understand them and that I needed sorely the gift of wisdom as I avidly sought for more instruction and information on the subject of spiritual gifts. I confess that in my over-enthusiasm in sharing the experience and searching for knowledge I inadvertently put off some friends. I ask their forgiveness. Someone has wisely said that one should try to keep silent for at least a year after experiencing the beginnings of the lesser gifts of the Holy Spirit until one has received the gift of the 'utterance of wisdom'! An unexpected series of visits to different parts of the world gave me an opportunity among other things of meeting such Anglican leaders as Archbishop Bill Burnett, then Bishop of Grahamstown, Graham Pulkingham, David Watson, Michael Harper and Dennis Bennett who assured me by word as well as by their first hand experiences that even Anglicans were being 'baptised in the Holy Spirit' and could also become instruments through which spiritual gifts could be distributed for the 'common good'! What we have experienced in these past years in Singapore together with what the various journeyings abroad were able to teach us about the Holy Spirit and the nature of 'spiritual gifts' and our seeing them in operation, has been invaluable. I would now like to share with you something of what we have learnt about the other spiritual gifts.

Operation of spiritual gifts

I believe that all spiritual gifts referred to in 1 Cor. 12: vv. 8–10 can be manifested through any child of God, for those who need that gift for their good, as the Holy Spirit wills. Naturally those who are more aware of the Holy Spirit's power and his willingness to manifest these gifts will be used more frequently as 'delivery boys'. Therefore all children of God should be ready at any time with expectation of healing to lay hands on and pray for those who are sick but to leave the outcome to the Lord. However, there are also those whom God has 'appointed' to particular ministries – for example – healing. St. Paul calls them 'healers' in 1 Cor. 12: v. 28. The Holy Spirit uses those people to give 'gifts of healing' more regularly and frequently. Or the person may be like the late Kathryn Kuhlman whom God 'appointed' a 'worker of miracles' so that miracles invariably were seen in her 'miracle services'. There are those like Agabus or the daughters of Philip in the Acts of the Apostles, whom God appointed to function as 'prophets'. In verses 28–30 of 1 Cor. 12: St. Paul is concerned about persons who have specialised ministries in the use of spiritual gifts in the Body of Christ. But in vv. 8–10 his focus is on the spiritual gifts themselves and how they may operate generally within the Body of Christ. It is in this latter sense that we shall look at the spiritual gifts.

Distinguishing between spirits

East Asia is an area where spirits are taken seriously. They are worshipped, invoked, placated, sought after to overcome other spirits through charms and counter charms. We find even some of the members of our churches, either through inadequate understanding or fear or merely as 'insurance' resorting to spirits and at the same time claiming to be practising Christians.

Soon after entering into the deeper experience of the Holy Spirit I felt a deep need to ask for the gift of distinguishing between spirits. I was asked by one who professed to be a member of our church to tell her if the spirits within her were of God. These spirits spoke to her each night revealing many hidden things accurately to her. Often they put her into trances. When in a trance she could heal all kinds of sicknesses and diseases but never in the name of Jesus. 'Why do you want to use the name of Jesus?' she asked. The spirits within her were able to 'slay' other spirits. She claimed to be a medium but only of 'good spirits'. Confrontation with those spirits showed us how accurate St. Paul was when he wrote that 'we are not contending against flesh and blood, but against principalities, against the powers, against the world rulers of this present darkness, against the spiritual hosts of wickedness in the heavenly places.' (Eph. 6: v. 12).

Sometimes we have to distinguish between ailments caused by a demonic spirit and those which have physical causes. We believe that close co-operation with the medical profession is needed and beneficial.

A Christian woman had suffered deafness in one ear for over two years. Her doctors had done all they could for her and asked her to come to our prayer and praise meeting. When we prayed for her nothing happened. I had a strong impression that this might be demonic activity. I asked her if at the time when she was stricken with deafness she had had any involvement with the occult or been to any temple. It was then that she recalled that she had accompanied a relative to a temple although she herself did nothing there. She was asked to confess this and then to renounce the particular spirit worshipped in that temple. She received her hearing back immediately after she had made the renunciation.

Sometimes there is a need to discern the kind of demonic spirit causing the bondage in order to set the person free. During the singing of the first hymn at a confirmation service, I became conscious of a raucous voice coming from the congregation. I found that it came from one of the candidates to be confirmed! He was foaming somewhat at the mouth with eyes closed, and as I went towards him the sounds changed into something like barks. I bound the spirit and commanded it to leave. All became quiet. When the hymn was restarted, however, the bark came back. After a few more unsuccessful attempts to cast the spirit out as the hymn proceeded I suddenly recalled that Graham Pulkingham had told me that 'religious spirits' were in their element during religious services, so I asked those around him to take him out while we proceeded with the service. A few days later in my private chapel with only two other clergy with me the 'religious spirit' left immediately it was commanded. The young man had never before been troubled in this way but had felt compelled to go from one religious sect to another. He has ceased to be troubled by this spirit, and is now a faithful Christian.

This experience showed me how important are the three questions addressed to baptism and confirmation candidates. I believe that it should be emphasised to each candidate that in answering these questions the candidate must in his spirit as well as with his lips renounce the devil and all his works, accept Jesus Christ as his personal Lord and Saviour and ask the Holy Spirit to come and fill his whole life and to empower him to live the Christian life. The renunciation is particularly important in our context because many of our adult candidates come from other religious backgrounds which involve spirit-worship.

We received a significant word of knowledge in this connection regarding Mark 16: v. 18 and Luke 10: v. 19 which has been helpful to us. It was revealed to us that the 'serpents and any deadly things' in our part of the world refer to charms and charmed drinks given out by mediums and temples. We have thus been able to assure our members that the promise of Our Lord covers and protects them. When they are inadvertently confronted by these evil things or have to drink that kind of poison they will not be hurt. This is important for our people as many of them have come from families some of whose members are practising spiritists.

Prophecy

My first lesson regarding this gift of the Spirit came when I visited Honolulu in 1973. I was invited to speak at the Evangelical Christian Church there. After I sat down the pastor surprised me by turning to me and saying in Elizabethan English:-

> Thou shalt find thyself, yea, entering into a ministry that thou hast not heretofore understood and thou hast partially held back from because of this, but the Lord shall deliver thee, yea, from all the fear that the enemy would try to bring upon thee. He shall strengthen thee mightily for surely the Lord opens before thee the door of utterance. Thou shalt minister by the Word of the Lord, yea, that which shall truly set the captive free, thou shalt minister.

Two others after him also spoke in Elizabethan English. I realised then that they were uttering prophecies concerning me.

At the end of the meeting a Japanese woman came up to

me and gave me a prophecy, this time by describing a vision which she had about me, which went as follows:-

> ... the Lord was going to use you as a plough. Somehow, as you were speaking about that work going on in that centre, I do not know in what relationship, but I saw, as you were speaking concerning the work, that God would use you as a plough that would be ploughing in the midst of this work that is going on. The other thought that came was that he would use you to thresh, by the strength of the Lord, the works of the enemy. It will be a God-given ministry and thou shalt go forth in the power and in the might and in the strength of the Lord.

Since then I have learnt that prophecy can come either through direct words – but not necessarily in Elizabethan English – at a public or private meeting, or it can also come vividly through visions. For example, recently while I was having an operation, a member of a group which was praying for me at the time, suddenly had a vision of me in the Lord's hands and being taken up gently and put back on my bed. She reported this to the group which responded with thanksgiving to the Lord. Within half an hour the group received a telephone message from the hospital, that I had come through the operation successfully and was now back in my ward bed.

I would also like to share what I believe to be a prophecy which I had on 2nd January 1974. I was praying in my chapel and asked the Lord to show me how he saw the whole continent of Asia. The words which suddenly came to my mind were 'The stone which the builders rejected has became the head of the corner.' (Luke 20: v. 17, Acts 4: v. 11). I pondered over the words and seemed to hear a voice saying 'I am the Head of the corner in Europe and the other continents, but I have been consistently rejected by the continent of Asia; but I have become the Head of the corner.'

I wondered how this could be when less than 1% are Christians in the whole of Asia. Later in the year I was to hear of the tremendous Expo 1974 in Seoul, where for one week one million Christians gathered for the evening meetings. Further news reached me of wonderful out-pourings of the Holy Spirit in so many countries in East Asia. I firmly believe that the Lord has become the Head of the corner in Asia and we shall see it happening.

The working of miracles

Though I had witnessed many healings at close quarters including some at meetings in my own house, I still could not be sure that the working of miracles was for today. A lady who had just come out from hospital after an operation came to stay with us. She could hardly walk, but the next night, after prayers for healing had been said for her, she stood up immediately and declared that the pain had left her and that she was completely healed. She proved it the next morning by going out to do her shopping in the city. It was still difficult for me to call that a miracle. There were scores of cases of people who immediately after they had been prayed for and told 'Be healed in the name of Jesus!' had received marked improvement in sight, or hearing, or walking. My problem was that there were still too many who did not become completely fit instantaneously. It was not until I attended the late Kathryn Kuhlman's 'Miracle Services' that I knew for a certainty that miracles do happen today through the power of the Holy Spirit. The Lord still remarkably confirms the preaching of his gospel with signs and wonders as he promised. (Mark 16: v. 20).

At one 'Miracle Service' where I was present, I saw arthritic patients who had spent many years in wheel-chairs, get out of them and walk up to the platform unaided. When Miss Kuhlman asked them to touch their toes, do knee-bends, jump up and down and run across the platform, they bent, jumped and ran with no difficulties whatsoever. A lame man who had come on crutches suddenly behaved like the one outside the Beautiful Gate when Peter told him to rise up and walk in the name of Jesus. He just jumped and leaped with joy as though he had never seen a crutch before. A blind lady who could not see at all before, began to read the small print in Miss Kuhlman's Bible. At another service a 10 year old girl who was blind because she had been born with a double cataract, suddenly could see clearly, when Miss Kuhlman, pointing in her direction in the balcony of the Shrine Auditorium, Los Angeles, told the congregation that 'some cataract had dropped'. Her mother gave the testimony of the miracle with tears of joy while the girl, wide-eyed, was taking in the whole beautiful scene through eyes that were able to see for the first time in her life! People gave testimonies from the stage that they had received 'impossible cures' and proved them in front of audiences of thousands by doing things impossible to them before. They were so like the miracles which Our Lord performed and are recorded in the Gospels. I can no longer accept the theory that they have to be 'demythologised'. Jesus Christ is the same yesterday, today and forever. The disciples saw miracles and so can we. He promised that 'he who believes in me will also do the works that I do; and greater works than these will he do, because I go to the Father.' (John 14: v. 12). And the promise is still being fulfilled. Miracles are for the twentieth century as well as the first.

I must admit that though I have witnessed so many

miracles in the U.S.A. and have read or heard reports of so many of them from all parts of the world, especially from Indonesia, and seen photos of them to prove them, I have seen only a few miracles of this dramatic kind in Singapore itself. We, however, look forward to the time when this gift will also be abundantly manifested by the Holy Spirit in our midst.

Utterance of knowledge

I believe that the word of knowledge came to me as I was studying Matt. 24 and the prophecies of our Lord regarding his second coming. As I read v. 14, 'This Gospel of the Kingdom will be preached throughout the world as a testimony of all . . . and then the end will come,' I thought, 'Well the end will be a long way off because this has hardly begun to be fulfilled in Asia.' Shortly after that, however, I was led to read Rev. 14: vv. 6 & 7: 'Then I saw another angel flying in mid-heaven, with an eternal Gospel to proclaim to those who dwell on earth, to every nation and tribe and tongue and people; and he said with a loud voice, "Fear God and give him glory, for the hour of his judgement has come; and worship him who made heaven and earth, the sea and the fountains of water." ' I saw the satellites orbiting the earth bouncing the Gospel message into all parts of the world including inaccessible parts of Asia. I began to see that these prophecies were being fulfilled and that we are living in the last days. I felt I needed confirmation.

Shortly afterwards I met George Otis, who made an unexpected visit to Singapore. When I shared these two passages with him he said he believed both the prophecies are now being fulfilled because the Gospel is being proclaimed to all parts of the world, even to the remotest

areas, by radio, TV directly or bounced off satellites. Later
Demos Shakarian whom the Lord used to found the Full
Gospel Businessmen Fellowship International, came to
Singapore and strengthened my conviction by telling me
that he had just completed contracts with broadcasting
companies which would beam Gospel messages to nearly
every part of the world.

I have often found it difficult to distinguish between
prophecy, interpretation of tongues, utterance of knowledge and utterance of wisdom. This is because all the gifts
are 'inspired by one and the same Spirit, who apportions to
each one individually as he wills.' (1 Cor. 12: v. 11). I believe
that we are not meant to analyse and clarify them too
neatly and correctly and so miss the wood for the trees.
William Law, seventeenth-century author of *Power of the
Spirit* has given one sentence which I find extremely helpful. 'God', he wrote, 'does not demand an unreasonable
faith but does demand a faith which goes beyond reason.'

What is clear is that the gifts which are given for the
'common good' are evidences of the sovereignty of God,
his love and compassion for the sufferer. An utterance of
knowledge concerning someone's marriage received and
given to the surprise of that person, who has been keeping
it a complete secret, shows to that person that God
knows, God loves her and that he is right beside her in her
problem and can see her through it if she will turn to him.
It also gives one the opportunity of being the person to
channel God's immense love to the sufferer. The miraculous utterances of knowledge which came through Kathryn
Kuhlman did not benefit Kathryn herself but set in motion
many spiritual gifts which benefit people suffering from not
only physical but also spiritual sicknesses. It matters little
precisely what spiritual gifts are in operation. What does

matter is that God in the person of the Holy Spirit is present and working for the good of his people. Where we come in is well expressed by St. Teresa of Avila: 'Christ has no body on earth but yours, no hands but yours, no feet but yours. Yours are the eyes through which Christ's compassion looks out on the world. Yours are the feet with which he goes about doing good. Yours are the hands with which he is to bless us now.'

Spiritual gifts and the ministry

What part can the spiritual gifts play in the ministry of the Church?

One day after this deeper experience of the Holy Spirit I was preparing a sermon, to be preached at a Holy Communion service, on Mark 7: vv. 31–37, the incident when Jesus healed the deaf and dumb man. Previously, I would have tried to give a rational explanation of how it could have taken place. However, since I had now seen the deaf receiving their hearing and so many miracles, I felt impelled to tell the congregation to take the record as it stands. Moreover, it occurred to me that when the record said 'and looking up to heaven, he (Jesus) sighed,' I believed that what the crowds heard as a sigh was Jesus praying to the Father in the Spirit. This appears to be confirmed by the incident in John 12: vv. 27–30 when Jesus prayed, 'Father, glorify thy Name,' a voice came from heaven, 'I have glorified it and will glorify it again,' but the crowd standing by said it was thunder. A more direct reference is Rom. 8: v. 26 'but the Spirit himself intercedes for us with sighs too deep for words.'

The point which I felt I had to make was that as Jesus when present performed miracles, so also whenever we see healings and miracles performed in the name of Jesus we knows that the Holy Spirit is present glorifying the name of Jesus. In the Holy Communion also our Lord and Saviour is specially present – 'His Spirit is with us.' At that moment I felt a question coming up within me. 'You know I will be present at the service. I want to see my children. Ask them to come after the service to the altar rails to meet me and receive my blessing through the minister of the church and yourself, as you lay hands on them.'

I had never issued an altar call before. Neither had there been an altar rail in that church before. I felt I could not disobey this inner voice. So with fear and trepidation but with the approval of the minister and not knowing what the response might be, I issued the call as part of the sermon. To the minister's surprise and mine, more than 30 remained behind after the service and came to the altar. The minister and I laid hands together on each of them and as we prayed in the Spirit to the Lord, his Spirit met their needs with spiritual gifts.

Since then it has become my practice whenever possible when I am officiating, to make an altar call and then together with the local minister, lay hands on and minister to those who have come up to the altar rails. I have found, first, that there are always at least a few who come forward for this further ministry. Secondly, those who come, invariably reveal their deepest need – be it rededication, commitment to Christ, doubts, healing, inner healing, deliverance – and the Lord meets them with the gifts of his Spirit to the glory of his Name. The benefits to those who responded to the call have been encouraging. For the ministers it has meant closer links with their people and the wonderful assurance that the spiritual gifts can operate through them too. For me, personally, being a channel for the Holy Spirit to manifest his gifts, has renewed and